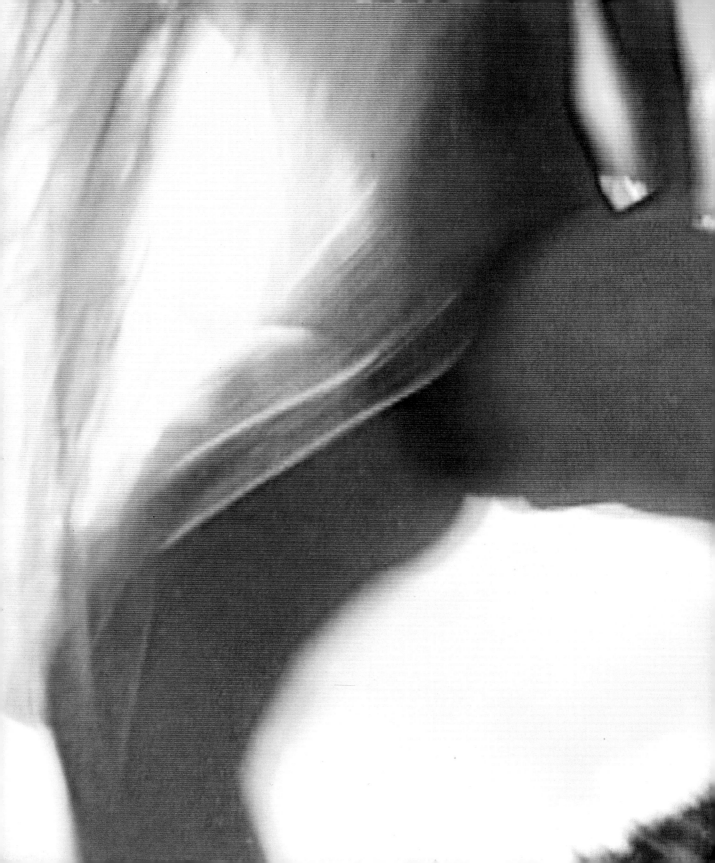

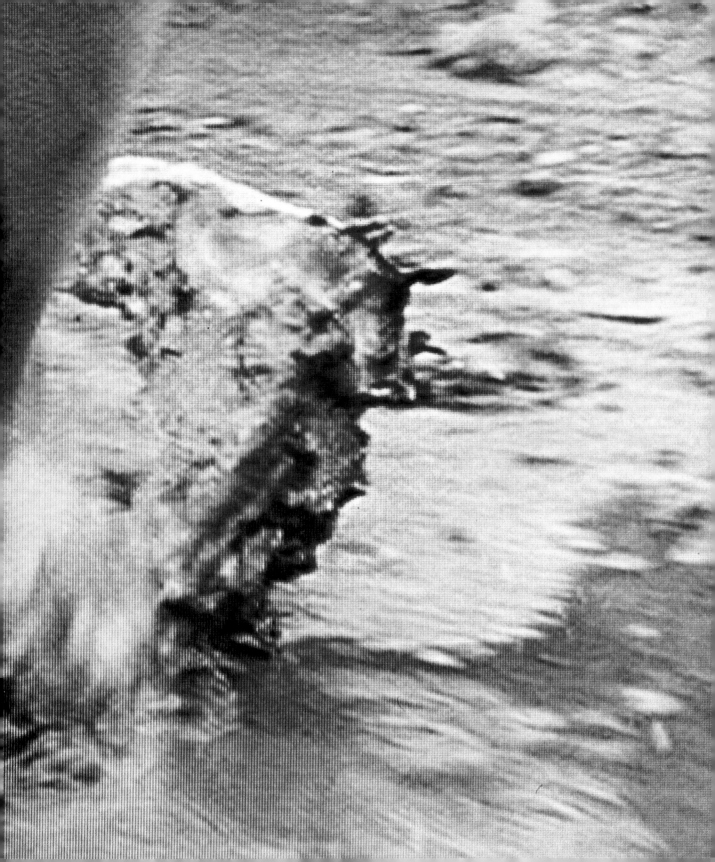

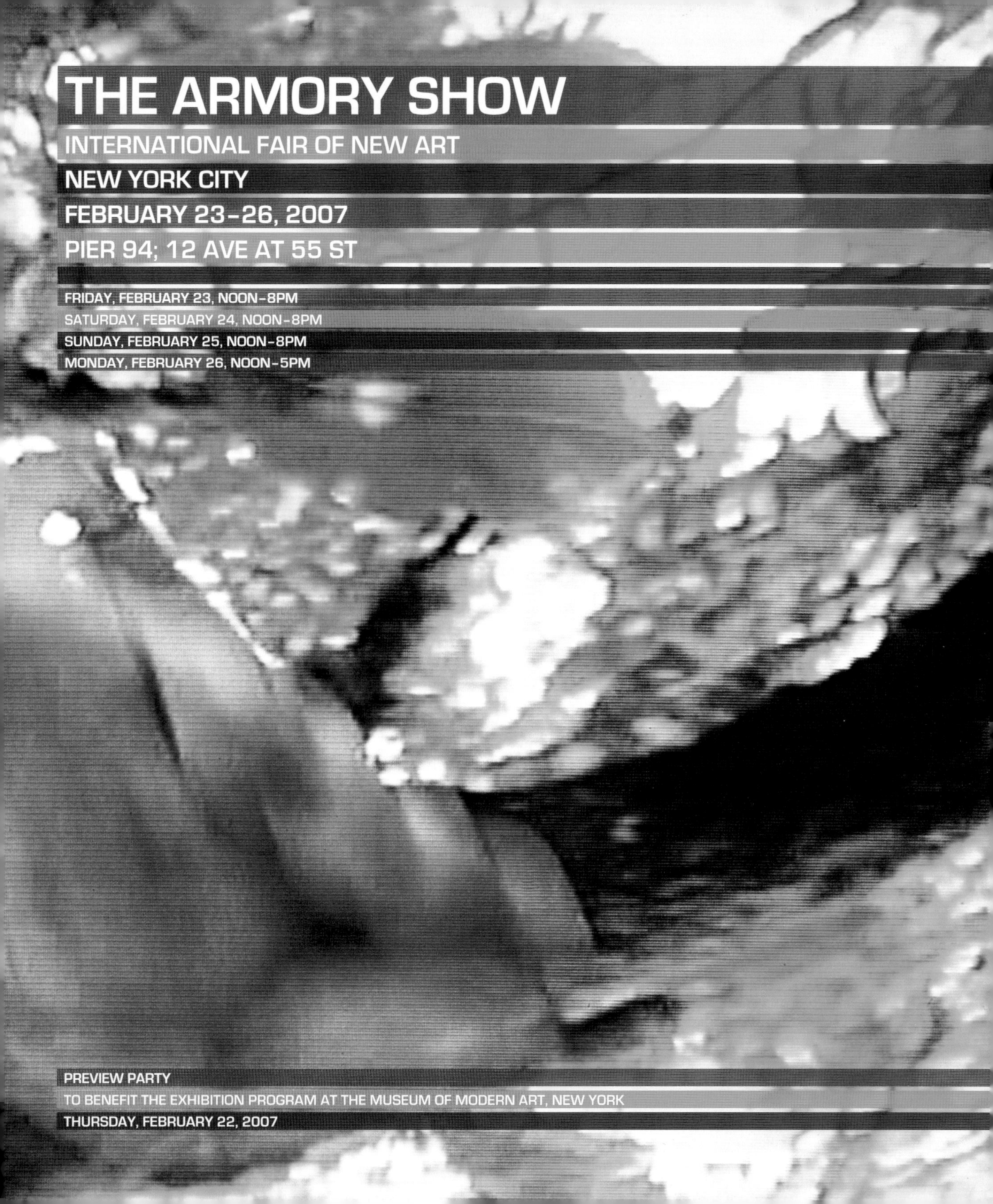

THE ARMORY SHOW

INTERNATIONAL FAIR OF NEW ART

NEW YORK CITY

FEBRUARY 23–26, 2007

PIER 94; 12 AVE AT 55 ST

FRIDAY, FEBRUARY 23, NOON–8PM

SATURDAY, FEBRUARY 24, NOON–8PM

SUNDAY, FEBRUARY 25, NOON–8PM

MONDAY, FEBRUARY 26, NOON–5PM

PREVIEW PARTY

TO BENEFIT THE EXHIBITION PROGRAM AT THE MUSEUM OF MODERN ART, NEW YORK

THURSDAY, FEBRUARY 22, 2007

THE CITY OF NEW YORK
OFFICE OF THE MAYOR
NEW YORK, NY 10007

February 23, 2007

Dear Friends:

It is a pleasure to welcome everyone to The Armory Show, The International Fair of New Art in New York City.

Since its introduction in 1999, The Armory Show has quickly become one of the world's leading art marketplaces, helping to fuel the City's economy and enhance our status as a top cultural destination. In its first year, the show attracted 8,000 visitors; last year, more than 47,000 attended, and galleries reported more than $62 million dollars in sales. Moreover, The Armory Show's dedication to presenting new art by living artists highlights the significant role emerging artists play in the contemporary art world and brings international prominence to New York's established and emerging artists communities.

I am delighted to welcome The Armory Show back for another exciting year. On behalf of the City of New York, please accept my best wishes for an enjoyable event and continued success.

Sincerely,

Michael R. Bloomberg
Mayor

I copulate with the sky
I scrape my bloodied finger slowly on loamy soil
The nail is a translucent curved keratin plate
firmly connected to a densly innervated nail bed to
scratch, crack and pull
Don't be afraid be mild
Nails of us primates consist of 100 to 150 irregular
one above the other laminated layers of horn cells
That is perfect, they simply lie there
You do not have to prove anything
We primates are divided into the two sub-orders of
wet- and dry-nosed apes which we are
You sound like light blue
There have been totally different concepts of eye
apparatus before our eyes have evolved (before
more 505'000'000 years)
You're not guilty unless you want to feel so

Eyes lounge embedded in a fat pad in the bone
sockets of the head of the meadow surrounded
with bulbous nerve strings to the brain masses
I can imagine to be more intelligent
I call you Bonsai with blood, a liver and eyes
The upper and the lower lids collide in the corners
The lower and the upper tear tubes each form small
tear holes – what a glory
Between them a black hole where the light occurs
the transparent cornea constantly flooded with tears
Body and spirit indivisible, not guilty
You're an accumulation of happy coincidences
over millions of years
Be mild please don't be scared
Eat from the fruits of wisdom
The glands around the lashes press out the eye
butter preventing an overflowing of tears
If I come too close to you
your lids would close by reflex
When something gets inside
it is out-washed by tears
The lids fold down like garbage container covers
Inside they are overgrown by conjunctiva
With other vertebrate animals the lid is transparent
and folds down like an eye protector too.

—PIPILOTTI RIST, NOVEMBER 2006

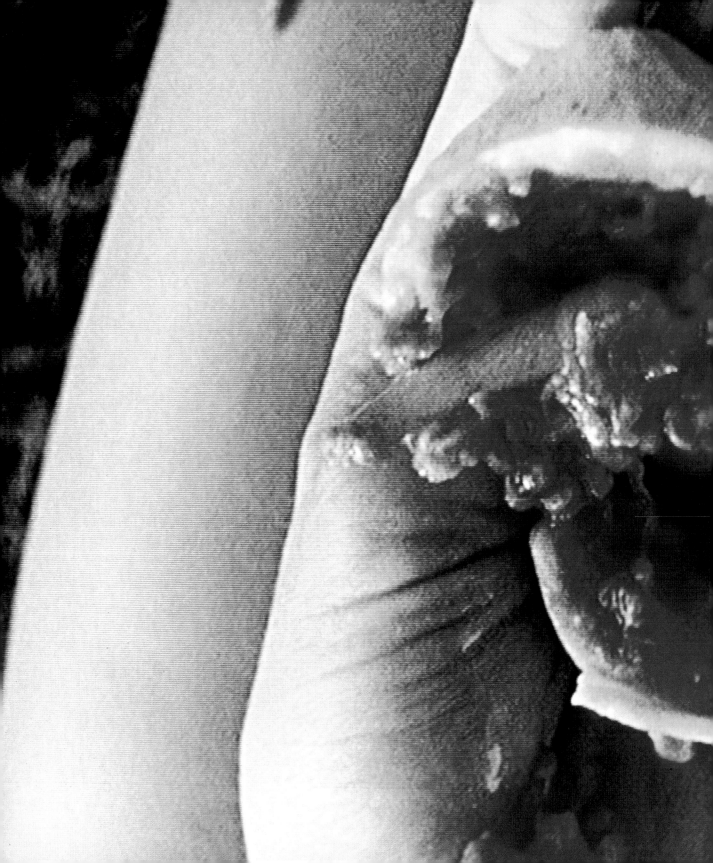

CLIFFORD CHANCE US LLP

31 WEST 52ND STREET
NEW YORK NY 10019 6131

TEL +1 212 878 8000
FAX +1 212 878 8375
www.cliffordchance.com

C L I F F O R D
C H A N C E

Dear Art Enthusiast:

Welcome to The Armory Show 2007.

As a global law firm, Clifford Chance is delighted to serve as Presenting Sponsor to the preeminent showcase for new art by living artists for the third consecutive year. We are proud to continue our relationship with our friends at the Armory Show. It's clear that the arts help to foster global communication and understanding. We see a strong link between the way in which we go about our international business, and the innovation and creativity the Show embodies.

Often using unconventional media, the artists showcased at the Armory Show engage their audiences in a unique way, taking multi-disciplinary approaches to appeal to the full range of human senses. Home to more collectors, galleries, critics and artists than any other city in the world, New York is well-suited to host this unique event. This year, the Armory Show will draw together the work of nearly 2000 artists, represented by 149 galleries in 44 cities around the world, making New York the true center of the international art world.

Clifford Chance is honored to be associated with The Armory Show. We take very seriously our longstanding commitment to sponsorship of the arts and other forms of community involvement.

We hope that you have a uniquely enjoyable experience.

Craig Medwick, Americas Regional Managing Partner

INTERNATIONAL
Herald Tribune
THE WORLD'S DAILY NEWSPAPER

ATELIER4

illy®

MANDARIN ORIENTAL
NEW YORK
SM

**CLIFFORD
CHANCE**

contemporary

New York

ARTFORUM

WPS1.ORG

QUINTESSENTIALLY

ARTUPDATE.COM/

vivavi

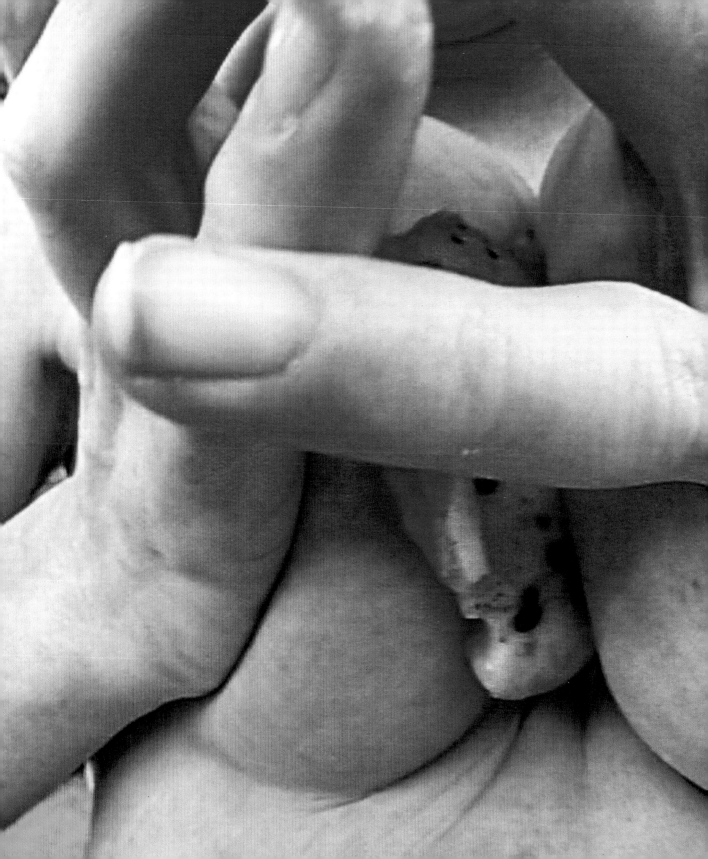

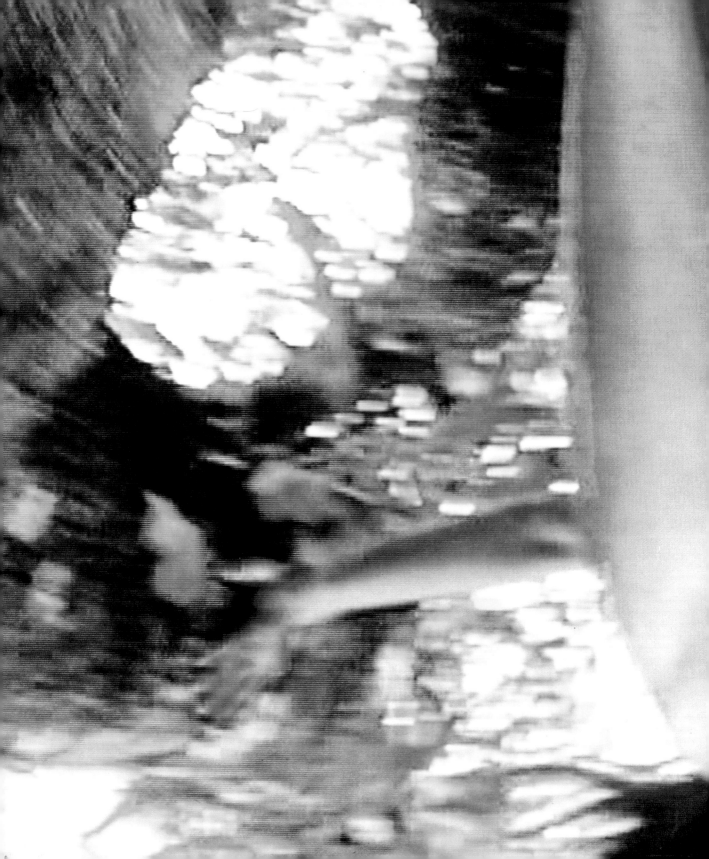

Exhibitors

AACHEN Adamski Gallery for Contemporary Art

AMSTERDAM Annet Gelink Gallery; Galerie Diana Stigter

ANTWERP Stella Lohaus Gallery; Zeno X Gallery

ATHENS The Breeder

BERLIN Arndt & Partner Berlin/Zurich; Galerie Guido W. Baudach; Galerie Crone; Galerie EIGEN + ART Leipzig/Berlin; Johann König; Galerie Aurel Scheibler; Galerie Thomas Schulte; Galerie Barbara Thumm; Galerie Barbara Weiss; Galerie Jan Wentrup; Jan Winkelmann/Berlin

BROOKLYN Pierogi

CAPE TOWN Michael Stevenson Gallery

CHICAGO Shane Campbell Gallery

CLUJ, ROMANIA Plan B

COLOGNE Galerie Christian Nagel; Johnen/Schöttle Cologne/Berlin/Munich

DRESDEN Galerie Gebr. Lehmann

DUBLIN Kerlin Gallery

DUSSELDORF Sies + Höke

GLASGOW Sorcha Dallas; The Modern Institute

HAMBURG Produzentengalerie Hamburg

ISTANBUL Galerist

KARLSRUHE Meyer Riegger Galerie

LONDON The Approach; Corvi-Mora; Thomas Dane Gallery; Dicksmith Gallery; Frith Street Gallery; greengrassi; Haunch of Venison; Herald St; Hotel; IBID Projects; Alison Jacques Gallery; Lisson Gallery; Victoria Miro Gallery; Maureen Paley; The Paragon Press; Stuart Shave/Modern Art; STORE; Sutton Lane; Timothy Taylor Gallery; Vilma Gold; White Cube/Jay Jopling

LOS ANGELES Angles Gallery; Black Dragon Society; Blum & Poe; China Art Objects; Marc Foxx; Anna Helwing Gallery; Daniel Hug; David Kordansky Gallery; Patrick Painter, Inc.; Peres Projects; Sandroni Rey; Richard Telles Fine Art

MADRID Galería Pepe Cobo

MEXICO Galería Enrique Guerrero

MIAMI Fredric Snitzer Gallery

MILAN Galleria Massimo De Carlo; francesca kaufmann

NAPLES Lia Rumma

NEW DELHI Nature Morte

NEW YORK 303 Gallery; Bellwether; Peter Blum Gallery; Marianne Boesky Gallery; Tanya Bonakdar Gallery; Bortolami Dayan; CANADA; Cheim & Read; James Cohan Gallery; John Connelly Presents; CRG Gallery; D'Amelio Terras; Deitch Projects; Ronald Feldman Fine Arts, Inc.; Zach Feuer Gallery; Foxy Production; Fredericks & Freiser; GERING LóPEZ Gallery; Greenberg Van Doren Gallery; Greene Naftali; Harris Lieberman; Casey Kaplan; Paul Kasmin Gallery; Sean Kelly Gallery; Anton Kern Gallery; Leo Koenig, Inc.; Andrew Kreps Gallery; Lehmann Maupin; Matthew Marks Gallery; Sara Meltzer Gallery; Metro Pictures; Robert Miller Gallery; Mitchell-Innes & Nash; Murray Guy; Carolina Nitsch; David Nolan Gallery; PaceWildenstein; Friedrich Petzel Gallery; The Project New York/Los Angeles; Daniel Reich Gallery; Rivington Arms; Jack Shainman Gallery; Taxter & Spengemann; Team Gallery; Wallspace; David Zwirner

OSAKA Kodama

PARIS Art : Concept; Galerie Chez Valentin; COSMIC Galerie; Galerie Chantal Crousel; in SITU; Yvon Lambert Paris/New York; Galerie Loevenbruck; Galerie Kamel Mennour; Galerie Emmanuel Perrotin; Galerie Praz-Delavallade; Galerie Almine Rech; Galerie Thaddaeus Ropac Paris/Salzburg

ROME Magazzino d'Arte Moderna

SAN FRANCISCO Jack Hanley Gallery

SAN GIMIGNANO Galleria Continua

SEOUL Arario Gallery; Kukje Gallery

STOCKHOLM Andréhn-Schiptjenko; Galleri Magnus Karlsson; Milliken

TEL-AVIV Sommer Contemporary Art

TOKYO Taka Ishii Gallery; Tomio Koyama Gallery; Shugoarts; Hiromi Yoshii

TURIN Galleria Franco Noero

VIENNA Georg Kargl; Galerie Krinzinger; Galerie Meyer Kainer

WEST PALM BEACH Gavlak

ZURICH Mai 36 Galerie; Galerie Eva Presenhuber; Hauser & Wirth Zurich London

303 Gallery

NEW YORK

ARTISTS

Doug Aitken
Laylah Ali
Anne Chu
Thomas Demand
Inka Essenhigh
Hans-Peter Feldmann
Ceal Floyer
Karel Funk
Maureen Gallace
Tim Gardner
Rodney Graham
Mary Heilmann
Karen Kilimnik
Florian Maier-Aichen
Kristin Oppenheim
Eva Rothschild

Collier Schorr
Stephen Shore
David Thorpe
Jane and Louise Wilson

ADDRESS

525 West 22nd Street
New York, NY 10011
USA
T: +1.212.255.1121
F: +1.212.255.1123
info@303gallery.com
www.303gallery.com

STAFF

Lisa Spellman
Mari Spirito
Simone Montemurno
Mariko Munro
Barbara Corti
Joann Kim
Kurt Brondo
Noam Rappaport
Simon Greenberg
Mike Rollins
Brian Doyle
Peter Owsiany
Rico Anderson
Jessica Graves Gonzales

Doug Aitken, **Film Stills from The Doug Aitken Project at MoMA** featuring untitled diamond neon sculpture, 2006, 72 x 52 inches; 185 x 132 cm

ARTISTS	ADDRESS	STAFF

ARTISTS

Edgar Arceneaux
Mariana Castillo Deball
Tobias & Raphael Danke
Lecia Dole Recio
Morgan Fisher
Charles Gaines
Frank Hesse
Achim Hoops
Olga Koumoundouros
Rodney McMillian
Stephan Moersch
Hans Niehus
Brian O'Connell
Alexander Rischer
Joel Tauber

ADDRESS

Passstrasse 14
D-52070 Aachen
GERMANY
T: +49.241.445.2550
F: +49.241.445.2551
mail@adamskigallery.com
www.adamskigallery.com

STAFF

Stefanie Maute, Director
Caroline Rordorf, Assistant
Stephan Adamski, Owner

Olga Koumoundouros, **O´s vs. I´s (Parity)**, 2006, Kevlar, foam beds, 182 x 47 x 24 inches; 460 x 120 x 60 cm

Andréhn-Schiptjenko

ARTISTS

Kader Attia
Uta Barth
Tommi Grönlund/
    Petteri Nisunen
Annika von Hausswolff
Meta Isæus-Berlin
Brad Kahlhamer
Anna Kleberg
Annika Larsson
Tony Matelli
Marilyn Minter
Zwelethu Mthethwa
Johan Nobell
Nina Saunders

Xavier Veilhan
Gunnel Wåhlstrand
Johan Zetterquist

ADDRESS

Markvardsgatan 2
S-11353 Stockholm
SWEDEN
T: +46.8.612.00.75
F: +46.8.612.00.76
info@andrehn-
    schiptjenko.com
www.andrehn-
    schiptjenko.com

STAFF

Ciléne Andréhn
Marina Schiptjenko
Elin Hagström
Robert Müller-Brunotte

Kader Attia, **Untitled**, 2006, ink on paper, 15 3/8 x 19 3/4 inches; 39 x 50 cm

Nina Saunders, **Refuge**, 2006, mixed media

Angles Gallery

SANTA MONICA

ARTISTS

Simone Adels
Polly Apfelbaum
Kevin Appel
Judie Bamber
Linda Besemer
Oliver Boberg
David Bunn
Jeremy Dickinson
Judy Fiskin
Ori Gersht
Tom LaDuke
Kelly McLane
Walter Niedermayr
Xiomara De Oliver
Adam Ross
Linda Stark

ADDRESS

2230 Main Street
Santa Monica, CA 90405
USA
T: +1.310.396.5019
F: +1.310.396.3797
info@anglesgallery.com
www.anglesgallery.com

2222 Main Street
Santa Monica, CA 90405
USA

STAFF

David McAuliffe,
    Owner/Director
Nowell J. Karten, Director
Minyoung Park,
    Associate Director

Kevin Appel, **Country Home 4 (Bridge)**, 2006, oil, enamel, acrylic on canvas over panel, 90 x 84 inches; 229 x 213 cm

The Approach

LONDON

ARTISTS

Haluk Akakçe
Phillip Allen
Cris Brodahl
Patrick Hill
Evan Holloway
Inventory
Germaine Kruip
Rezi van Lankveld
Dave Muller
Jacques Nimki
Michael Raedecker
Brett Cody Rogers
John Stezaker
Mari Sunna
Evren Tekinoktay

Gary Webb
Martin Westwood
Tom Wood
Shizuka Yokomizo

ADDRESS

1st Floor
47 Approach Road
E2 9LY London
UNITED KINGDOM
T: +44.208.983.3878
F: +44.208.983.3919
info@theapproach.co.uk
www.theapproach.co.uk

2nd Floor
336 Old Street
EC1V 9DR London
UNITED KINGDOM
T: +44.207.729.2629
F: +44.208.983.3919
info@thereliance.co.uk
www.thereliance.co.uk

STAFF

Jake Miller
Emma Robertson
Mike Allen
Vanessa Carlos

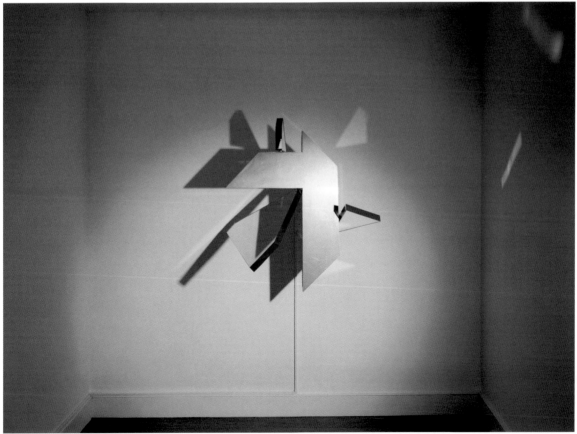

Germaine Kruip, **Counter Composition**, 2006, Edition of 3, mirror, wood, stainless steel, mechanics, 31 1/2 x 31 1/2 x 31 1/2 inches; 80 x 80 x 80 cm

Arario Gallery

ARTISTS

Hyunjhin Baik
Suejin Chung
Wang Guangyi
Osang Gwon
Zeng Hao
Joonho Jeon
Sui Jianguo
Liu Jianhua
Jitish Kallat
Hyungkoo Kang
Bharti Kher
Hanna Kim
Inbae Kim
Sunghyun Kyung
Donghee Koo
Tallur L.N
Hyungkoo Lee
Dongwook Lee

Jinyong Lee
Ji-hyun Lee
Seungae Lee
Yongbaek Lee
Fang Lijun
Yue Minjun
Sejin Park
Justin Ponmany
Yang Shaobin

ADDRESS

#354-1, Shinbu-dong,
Cheonan-si
Chungcheongnam-do
110-200 Seoul
KOREA
T: +82.41.551.5100
F: +82.41.551.5102

Jiuchang Art Complex
Beihuqu Road
Anwaibeiyuan Street
Chaoyang District
100012 Beijing
P.R. CHINA
T: +86.10.5202.3803
F: +86.10.5202.3808
juney@arario.com
www.arariogallery.com

STAFF

Cheagab Yun,
    Director, Beijing
Henna Joo,
    Director, Cheonan
Jane Yoon,
    Director, Seoul

Wang, Guangyi, **Great Criticism - Cohiba**, 2005, oil on canvas, 118 x 236 1/6 inches; 300 x 600 cm

Hyungkoo Lee, **Lepus Animatus**, 2005-2006, resin, aluminum sticks, stainless steel wires, springs and oil paint, 43 3/4 x 23 2/3 x 27 2/3 inches / 111 x 60 x 70 cm

Zeng Hao, **Noon**, 16, June 2001, oil on canvas, 118 x 94 1/2 inches; 300 x 240 cm

Arndt & Partner

BERLIN/ZURICH

ARTISTS

Adam Adach
Jules de Balincourt
Florian Baudrexel
Sue de Beer
Sophie Calle
William Cordova
Yannick Demmerle
Torben Giehler
Gabi Hamm
Anton Henning
Mathilde ter Heijne
Thomas Hirschhorn
Henning Kles
Douglas Kolk
Karsten Konrad

Yayoi Kusama
Josephine Meckseper
Muntean/Rosenblum
Tam Ochiai
Erik Parker
Julian Rosefeldt
Lisa Ruyter
Charles Sandison
Dennis Scholl
Nedko Solakov
Hiroshi Sugito
Tim Trantenroth
Susan Turcot
Veron Urdarianu

ADDRESS

Arndt & Partner Berlin
Zimmerstrasse 90 - 91
D-10117 Berlin
GERMANY
T: +49.30.280.8123
F: +49.30.283.3738
arndt@andt-partner.com
www.arndt-partner.com

Arndt & Partner Zurich
Lessingstrasse 5
CH-8002 Zurich
SWITZERLAND
T: +41.43.817.6780
F: +41.43.817.6782
zurich@arndt-partner.com
www.arndt-partner.com

STAFF

Matthias Arndt
Thorsten Albertz
Julie Burchardi
Anna Lemke Duque
Natalija Martinovic

William Cordova, **Arrow of god (4-chinna achebe)**, detail, 2006, pencil on paper, 127 x 260.5 cm

ARTISTS	ADDRESS	STAFF
Pierre-Olivier Arnaud	16, rue Duchefdelaville	Olivier Antoine
Julien Audebert	F-75013 Paris	Daniele Balice
Nathan Hylden	FRANCE	Caroline Maestrali
Gedi Sibony	T: +33.1.53.60.90.30	
Roman Signer	F: +33.1.53.60.90.31	
	info@galerieartconcept.com	
	www.galerieartconcept.com	

Roman Signer, **Kayak**, 2005, barrel, cut kayak, pump, 51 x 24 x 12 inches; 130 x 60 x 30 cm

Galerie Guido W. Baudach   BERLIN

ARTISTS	ADDRESS	STAFF

ARTISTS

André Butzer
Björn Dahlem
Thilo Heinzmann
Thomas Helbig
Andreas Hofer
Erwin Kneihsl
Bjarne Melgaard
Markus Selg
Thomas Zipp

ADDRESS

Oudenarder Strasse 16-20
D-13347 Berlin
GERMANY
T: +49.30.280.47.727
F: +49.30.280.47.727
galerie@guidowbaudach.com
www.guidowbaudach.com

STAFF

Guido W. Baudach
Heike Tosun
Berit Homburg
Katrin Rother

Andreas Hofer, **Tomorrow People**, 2004, acrylic / lacquer on wood, 110 1/6 x 1771/6 inches; 280 x 450 cm

Bellwether

NEW YORK

ARTISTS

Ellen Altfest
John Bauer
Tanyth Berkeley
Clayton Brothers
Adam Cvijanovic
Brent Green
Everest Hall
Kirsten Hassenfeld
Jocelyn Hobbie
Trevor Paglen
Allison Smith
Marc Swanson
Amy Wilson

ADDRESS

134 10th Avenue
New York, NY 10011
USA
T: +1.212.929.5959
F: +1.212.929.5912
info@bellwethergallery.com
www.bellwethergallery.com

STAFF

Becky Smith
Erica Samuels
Kristina Ernst

Trevor Paglen, **Unmarked 737 at 'Gold Coast' Terminal/Las Vegas, NV/Distance ~1 mile/10:44 pm**, 2005, C-print

Black Dragon Society   LOS ANGELES

ARTISTS

Steve Canaday
Gerald Davis
Bart Exposito
Hannah Greely
Gustavo Herrera
Elisa Johns
Raffi Kalenderian
Charles Karubian
Julie Kirkpatrick
Nick Lowe
Jodie Mohr
Pentti Monkkonen
Juliana Paciulli
Tia Pulitzer
Ry Rocklen

Rob Thom
Philip Wagner
Jonas Wood

ADDRESS

961 Chung King Road
Los Angeles, CA 90012
USA
T: +1.213.620.0030
F: +1.213.620.0028
info@Black-Dragon-
    Society.com
www.Black-Dragon-
    Society.com

971 Chung King Road
Los Angeles, CA 90012
USA
T: +1.213.620.0030
F: +1.213.620.0028

STAFF

Parker Jones
Cammie Staros
Roger Herman
Hubert Schmalix
Chris Sievernich

Philip Wagner, **Drift**, 2006, mixed media on canvas, 96 x 78 inches; 244 x 198 cm

ARTISTS

Chiho Aoshima
Tatsurou Bashi
Jennifer Bornstein
Slater Bradley
Pierpaolo Campanini
Nigel Cooke
Sam Durant
Anya Gallaccio
Mark Grotjahn
Julian Hoeber
Matt Johnson
Friedrich Kunath

Sharon Lockhart
Florian Maier-Aichen
Dave Muller
Takashi Murakami
Yoshitomo Nara
Hirsch Perlman
Dirk Skreber
Chris Vasell

ADDRESS

2754 S. La Cienega Blvd.
Los Angeles, CA 90034
USA
T: +1.310.836.2062
F: +1.310.836.2104
info@blumandpoe.com
www.blumandpoe.com

STAFF

Timothy Blum, Owner
Jeffrey Poe, Owner
Silke Taprogge, Director

Julian Hoeber, **Take a Walk, Motherfucker**, 2006 (detail), gouache, acrylic and graphite on paper; 7 1/2 x 161 inches; 19 x 409 cm

Peter Blum Gallery

ARTISTS	ADDRESS	STAFF
John Beech	99 Wooster Street	Peter Blum
Louise Bourgeois	New York, NY 10012	Simone Subal
Rudolf de Crignis	USA	Yana Balson
Helmut Federle	T: +1.212.343.0441	Robert Jack
Suzan Frecon	F: +1.212.343.0523	Rebekah Beaver
Simon Frost	soho@peterblumgallery.com	Michael Homer
Josephsohn	www.peterblumgallery.com	Hannah Gibson
Alex Katz		
Kimsooja	526 West 29th Street	
Joseph Marioni	New York, NY 10001	
Chris Marker	USA	
David Rabinowitch	T: +1.212.244.6055	
Su-Mei Tse	F: +1.212.244.6054	
Robert Zandvliet	chelsea@peterblum	
	gallery.com	
	www.peterblumgallery.com	

Kimsooja, **A Wind Woman**, 2003-2006, Unique Iris print, 35 x 47 inches; 89 x 119.5cm

Chris Marker, **Athos 2**, b/w photograph

Marianne Boesky Gallery

NEW YORK

ARTISTS

Kevin Appel
Chinatsu Ban
Yi Chen
Liz Craft
Sue de Beer
Stephanie Dost
Martin Eder
Rachel Feinstein
Thomas Flechtner
Barnaby Furnas
Jay Heikes
Adam Helms
Franziska Holstein
Mary Ellen Mark
Donald Moffett
Takashi Murakami

Yoshitomo Nara
Jacco Olivier
Alexander Ross
Sarah Sze
Kon Trubkovich
Hannah van Bart
John Waters
Ivette Zighelboim

ADDRESS

509 West 24th Street
New York, NY 10011
USA
T: +1.212.680.9889
F: +1.212.680.9897
info@marianneboesky
    gallery.com
www.marianneboesky
    gallery.com

STAFF

Marianne Boesky
Elisabeth Ivers
Adrian Turner
Amy Greenspon
Annie Rana

Hannah van Bart, **Untitled**, 2006, acrylic on canvas, 65 x 59 1/8 inches; 165 x 150 cm

Tanya Bonakdar Gallery

NEW YORK

ARTISTS

Uta Barth
Martin Boyce
Sandra Cinto
Phil Collins
Mat Collishaw
Mark Dion
Olafur Eliasson
Michael Elmgreen/
   Ingar Dragset
Siobhán Hapaska
Sabine Hornig
Teresa Hubbard/
   Alexander Birchler
Ian Kiaer
Carla Klein
Atelier van Lieshout
Charles Long
Mark Manders

Jason Meadows
Ernesto Neto
Rivane Neuenschwander
Peggy Preheim
Thomas Scheibitz
Hannah Starkey
Dirk Stewen
Nicole Wermers

ADDRESS

521 West 21st Street
New York, NY 10011
USA
T: +1.212.414.4144
F: +1.212.414.1535
mail@tanyabonakdar
   gallery.com
www.tanyabonakdar
   gallery.com

STAFF

Tanya Bonakdar,
   Founder/Director
Ethan Sklar, Director
James Lavender, Director

Thomas Scheibitz, **Mary**, 2006, oil on linen, 118 x 74 3/4 inches; 300 x 190 cm

Bortolami Dayan

NEW YORK

ARTISTS

Hope Atherton
Avner Ben-Gal
Daniel Buren
Michel François
Piero Golia
Thomas Helbig
Scott King
Luigi Ontani
Patrick Tuttofuoco
Gary Webb
Eric Wesley

ADDRESS

510 West 25th Street
New York, NY 10001
USA
T: +1.212.727.2050
F: +1.212.727.2060
info@bortolamidayan.com
www.bortolamidayan.com

STAFF

Stefania Bortolami
Amalia Dayan
Elizabeth Schwartz
Gordon Christmas
Will Richmond-Watson

Avner Ben-Gal, **Untitled**, 2006, acrylic on paper, 39 x 27 1/2 inches; 99.1 x 69.9 cm

The Breeder   ATHENS

ARTISTS

Markus Amm
Athanasios Argianas
Marc Bijl
Matt Connors
Iris Van Dongen
Vasso Gavaisse
Uwe Henneken
Dionisis Kavallieratos
Scott Myles
Ilias Papailiakis
Mindy Shapero
Gert & Uwe Tobias
Alexandros Tzannis
Jannis Varelas
Vangelis Vlahos

ADDRESS

6, Evmorfopoulou St.
GR-10553 Athens
GREECE
T: +30.210.331.7527
F: +30.210.331.7527
gallery@thebreeder
   system.com
www.thebreedersystem.com

STAFF

Stathis Panagoulis
George Vamvakidis
Natasha Adamou

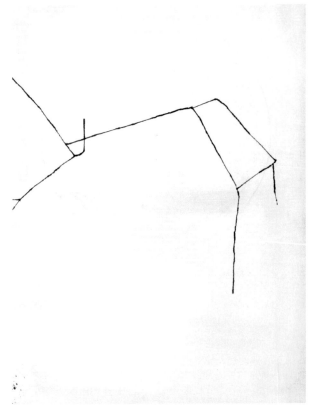

Markus Amm, **Untitled**, 2005, oil, ink, graphite on linen canvas, 39 3/8 x 31 1/2 inches; 100 x 80 cm

Shane Campbell Gallery

ARTISTS

Jesse Chapman
Pete Fagundo
Kim Fisher
Michelle Grabner
Joanne Greenbaum
Mark Grotjahn
Carrie Gundersdorf
Jay Heikes
Patrick Hill
Alice Könitz
Suzanne McClelland
Jason Meadows
Rebecca Morris

Aliza Nisenbaum
William J. O'Brien
Anthony Pearson
Noah Rorem
Elizabeth Saveri
Chris Vasell
Mary Weatherford

ADDRESS

1431 West Chicago Avenue
Chicago, IL 60622
USA
T: +1.312.226.2223
shane@shanecampbell
  gallery.com
www.shanecampbell
  gallery.com

125 North Harvey Avenue
Oak Park, IL 60302
USA
T: +1.630.697.0609

STAFF

Shane Campbell
Julie Campbell
Tania Torres-Sanchez
Laura Mackin

Anthony Pearson, **Shalamar (straight)**, 2005, solarized silver gelatin print, 6 x 4.75 inches; 15 x 12 cm

CANADA   NEW YORK

ARTISTS

David Askevold
Devendra Banhart
Brian Belott
Katherine Bernhardt
Joe Bradley
Sarah Braman
Rosson Crow
Phil Grauer
Xylor Jane
Tom Johnson
Lily Ludlow
Michael Mahalchick
Frankie Martin
Carrie Moyer

Luke Murphy
Elena Pankova
Robin Peck
Jocelyn Shipley
Anke Weyer
Wallace Whitney

ADDRESS

55 Chrystie Street
New York, NY 10002
USA
T: +1.212.925.4631
gallery@canadanew
   york.com
www.canadanewyork.com

STAFF

Suzanne Butler
Sarah Braman
Phil Grauer
Wallace Whitney

Rosson Crow, **Silent Rooms with Carpets So Heavy All Footsteps Are Absorbed**, 2006, oil on canvas, 77 x 90 inches; 196 x 229 cm

Cheim & Read

NEW YORK

ARTISTS

Donald Baechler
Jean-Michel Basquiat
Lynda Benglis
Louise Bourgeois
Richmond Burton
William Eggleston
Louise Fishman
Adam Fuss
Jenny Holzer
Bill Jensen
Jannis Kounellis
Jonathan Lasker
McDermott & McGough
Joan Mitchell
Paul Morrison

Jack Pierson
Monique Prieto
Alessandro Raho
John Sonsini
Pat Steir
Juan Uslé

ADDRESS

547 West 25th Street
New York, NY 10001
USA
T: +1.212.242.7727
F: +1.212.242.7737
gallery@cheimread.com
www.cheimread.com

STAFF

John Cheim
Howard Read
Mary Parr
Adam Sheffer

John Sonsini, **FERNANDO, MANUEL, DAVID**, 2006, oil on canvas, 80 x 96 inches; 203.2 x 243.8 cm

Galerie Chez Valentin

PARIS

ARTISTS

Pierre Ardouvin
Eric Baudart
Etienne Bossut
Véronique Boudier
Franck David
Olivier Dollinger
Babak Ghazi
Laurent Grasso
Yves Grenet
Carlos Kusnir
Mathieu Mercier
Nicolas Moulin
François Nougiès
David Renggli
Jean-Michael Sanejouand

Joe Scanlan
Gitte Schäfer
Veit Stratmann

ADDRESS

9, rue Saint Gilles
F-75003 Paris
FRANCE
T: +33.1.4887.4255
F: +33.1.4887.4435
galeriechezvalentin@noos.fr
www.galeriechezvalen
  tin.com

STAFF

Philippe Valentin, Director
Fréderique Valentin,
  Director
Joseph Tang, Assistant
Jessica Hakoun, Assistant

Mathieu Mercier, **Untitled**, 2006, painted metal, 134 x 43 x 15 3/4 inches; 340 x 109 x 40cm

China Art Objects

LOS ANGELES

ARTISTS

Andy Alexander
Walead Beshty
Bjorn Copeland
Kim Fisher
Morgan Fisher
Thomas Helbig
David Korty
Sean Landers
Ruby Neri
JP Munro
Andy Ouchi
Oliver Payne & Nick Relph
Jonathan Pylypchuk
Eric Wesley
Pae White
TJ Wilcox

ADDRESS

933 Chung King Road
Los Angeles, CA 90012
USA
T: +1.213.613.0384
F: +1.213.613.0363
info@chinaartobjects.com
www.chinaartobjects.com

STAFF

Steven Hanson
Maeghan Reid
Amy Yao

Walead Beshty, **Pictures Made By My Hand With the Assistance of Light**, 2006, b/w photogram on fiber based gelatin silver paper, 44 x 77 inches; 112 x 196 cm

Galería Pepe Cobo

MADRID

ARTISTS

Ibon Aranberri
John Baldessari
Stephan Balkenhol
Joan Cardells
Willie Doherty
Pepe Espaliú
Federico Guzmán
Diango Hernández
Cristina Iglesias
Rinko Kawauchi
Zoe Leonard
Juan Muñoz
Gonzalo Puch
MP & MP Rosado

Glen Rubsamen
Julião Sarmento
Ann-Sofi Sidén
Joel Sternfeld
Augustina von Nagel

ADDRESS

Galería Pepe Cobo
C/ Fortuny, 39 - Bajo Dcha
E-28010 Madrid
SPAIN
T: +34.91.319.0683
F: +34.91.308.3190
info@pepecobo.com
www.pepecobo.com

STAFF

José Cobo, Director
Sara Martín Prat
Luisa Bernal
Isabel Garcia de Castro

Gonzalo Puch, **Untitled**, 2006, color digital print, 51 1/6 x 41 inches; 130 x 103.85 cm

James Cohan Gallery

NEW YORK

ARTISTS

Manfredi Beninati
Ingrid Calame
Trenton Doyle Hancock
Folkert de Jong
Yun-Fei Ji
Richard Long
Beatriz Milhazes
Ron Mueck
Bill Owens
Roxy Paine
Richard Patterson
Alan Saret
Hiraki Sawa
Yinka Shonibare
The Estate of
    Robert Smithson

Erick Swenson
Tabaimo
Alison Elizabeth Taylor
Fred Tomaselli
Bill Viola
Wim Wenders

ADDRESS

533 West 26th Street
New York, NY 10001
USA
T: +1.212.714.9500
F: +1.212.714.9510
info@jamescohan.com
www.jamescohan.com

STAFF

James Cohan
Elyse Goldberg
Arthur Solway

Folkert de Jong, **Chop Chair**, 2005, styrofoam, polyurethane foam, silicone rubber, 35 x 30 3/4 x 43 3/4 inches; 89 x 78 x 111 cm

John Connelly Presents

NEW YORK

ARTISTS

assume vivid astro focus
Marco Boggio Sella
AA Bronson
Gerald Davis
Kaye Donachie
Kim Fisher
Freeman/Phelan
Kent Henricksen
Scott Hug
Alex Kwartler
Nick Lowe
Andrew Mania
Gerard Maynard
Philippe Perrot
Ara Peterson
Justin Samson
Mungo Thomson
Althea Thauberger

Scott Treleaven
Michael Wetzel
Grant Worth

ADDRESS

625 West 27th Street
New York, NY 10001
USA
T: +1.212.337.9563
F: +1.212.337.9613
info@johnconnellypresents.
  com
www.johnconnellypresents.
  com

STAFF

John Connelly,
  Owner & Director
Thea McKenzie,
  Associate Director
Jarrod Anderson,
  Registrar & Preparator
Joanne Kim,
  Gallery Archivist

Michael Wetzel, **Monkey Island II**, 2006, oil and egg tempera on canvas, 22 x 25 inches; 56 x 64 cm

Galleria Continua

ARTISTS

Hans Op de Beeck
Daniel Buren
Letizia Cariello
Loris Cecchini
Chen Zhen
Berlinde De Bruyckere
Carlos Garaicoa
Kendell Geers
Mona Hatoum
Ilya Kabakov
Anish Kapoor
Jorge Macchi
Sabrina Mezzaqui
Moataz Nasr
Lucy Orta
Luca Pancrazzi
Bruno Peinado
Michelangelo Pistoletto

Nedko Solakov
Pascale Marthine Tayou

ADDRESS

Via del Castello, 11
I-53037 San Gimignano
ITALY
T: +39.0577.943134
F: +39.0577.940484
info@galleriacontinua.com
www.galleriacontinua.com

Dashanzi 798 #8503
2 Jiuxianqiao Road
Chaoyang Dst.
100015 Beijing
CHINA
T: +86.10.64361005
F: +86.10.64364464
beijing@galleriacontinua.com

STAFF

Mario Cristiani, Director
Lorenzo Fiaschi, Director
Marurizio Rigillo, Director
Federica Beltrame, Director

Loris Cecchini, **Cloudless**, 2006, 12 aluminum ladders, steel wires, 50,000 plastic balls, fixing plastic strips, variable dimensions, installation view at Galleria Continua, Beijing, 2006, Ph. Zhao Zhao

Corvi-Mora

LONDON

ARTISTS

Richard Aldrich
Abel Auer
Brian Calvin
Pierpaolo Campanini
Anne Collier
Andy Collins
Rachel Feinstein
Dee Ferris
Liam Gillick
Richard Hawkins
Roger Hiorns
Jim Isermann
Colter Jacobsen
Dorota Jurczak
Aisha Khalid
Armin Krämer

Eva Marisaldi
Jason Meadows
Monique Prieto
Muhammad Imran Qureshi
Andrea Salvino
Glenn Sorensen
Tomoaki Suzuki

ADDRESS

1a Kempsford Road
SE11 4NU London
UNITED KINGDOM
T: +44.207.840.9111
F: +44.207.840.9112
info@corvi-mora.com
www.corvi-mora.com

STAFF

Tommaso Corvi-Mora
Tabitha Langton-Lockton

Auer Auer, **Installation View**, April-May 2006

Cosmic Gallery

PARIS

ARTISTS

Haluk Akakçe
Gilles Balmet
Vanessa Beecroft
Laetitia Benat
Tobias Bernstrup
Marc Bijl
Marco Boggio Sella
Pierre Bismuth
Benoît Broisat
Kimberly Clark
Mat Collishaw
Aurélien Froment
Piero Golia
James Hopkins
Christian Jankowski
Annika Larsson
Miltos Manetas
Maria Marshall

Gianni Motti
Iris Van Dongen
Richard Woods

ADDRESS

7 - 9, rue de l'Équerre
F-75019 Paris
FRANCE
T: +33.1.42.71.72.73
F: +33.1.42.71.72.00
contact@cosmicgalerie.com
www.cosmicgalerie.com

STAFF

Claudia Cargnel,
    Owner/Director
Frédéric Bugada,
    Owner/Director

Iris van Dongen, **Hooligan IV**, 2006, pencil, pastel, watercolor, charcoal on paper, 100 3/4 x 59 inches; 256 x 150 cm

ARTISTS

Robert Beck
Rhona Bitner
Russell Crotty
Tomory Dodge
Robert Feintuch
Pia Fries
Ori Gersht
Lyle Ashton Harris
Jim Hodges
Butt Johnson
Siobhan Liddell
Melissa McGill
Kelly McLane
Stephanie Pryor
Sam Reveles

Jeffrey Saldinger
Lisa Sanditz
Sandra Scolnik
Mindy Shapero
Frances Stark

ADDRESS

535 West 22nd Street
New York, NY 10011
USA
T: +1.212.229.2766
F: +1.212.229.2788
mail@crggallery.com
www.crggallery.com

STAFF

Carla Chammas,
   Owner/Director
Richard Desroche,
   Owner/Director
Glenn McMillan,
   Owner/Director
Alex Dodge, Director
Glen Baldridge, Director

Butt Johnson, **Unrequited Love**, 2003-2005, ballpoint pen on paper, 24 x 36 inches; 61 x 91 cm

Galerie Crone

BERLIN

ARTISTS

Ena Swansea
Rosemarie Trockel
Hanne Darboven
Almut Heise
Amelie von Wulffen

ADDRESS

Kochstraße 60
D-10969 Berlin
GERMANY
T: +49.30.2589.9370
F: +49.30.2589.9371
info@cronegalerie.de
www.cronegalerie.de

STAFF

Andreas Osarek
Axel Benz
Evelyn Marwehe
Wiebke Neumann

Amelie von Wulffen, **AvW06-C016 Ohne Titel**, 2006, acrylic, watercolour, photograph, charcoal on paper, 66 1/2 x 59 1/10 inches; 169 x 150 cm

Galerie Chantal Crousel

PARIS

ARTISTS

Jennifer Allora &
    Guillermo Calzadilla
Darren Almond
Fikret Atay
Tony Cragg
Fabrice Gygi
Mona Hatoum
Thomas Hirschhorn
Hassan Khan
Michael Krebber
Jean-Luc Moulène
Moshe Ninio
Melik Ohanian
Gabriel Orozco
Anri Sala

Alain Séchas
José Maria Sicilia
Sean Snyder
Reena Spaulings
Rirkrit Tiravanija

ADDRESS

10, Rue Charlot
F-75003 Paris
FRANCE
T: +33.1.42.77.38.87
F: +33.1.42.77.59.00
galerie@crousel.com
www.crousel.com

STAFF

Chantal Crousel
Niklas Svennung

Thomas Hirschhorn, **Clous-Mannequin (rangée)**, 2006, 8 models painted, nails, screws, tapes, 74 3/4 x 110 1/6 x 47 1/6 inches; 190 x 280 x 120 cm
Exhibition view: "Concretion", Le Creux de l'Enfer, Thiers, 2006

D'Amelio Terras

NEW YORK

ARTISTS

Adam Adach
Whitney Bedford
Delia Brown
Case Calkins
Tony Feher
Amy Globus
Joanne Greenbaum
Matt Keegan
Kim Krans
John Morris
Rei Naito
Noguchi Rika
Cornelia Parker
Dario Robleto
Heather Rowe
Karin Sander

Noah Sheldon
Yoshihiro Suda
Sara VanDerBeek

ADDRESS

525 West 22nd Street
New York, NY 10011
USA
T: +1.212.352.9460
F: +1.212.352.9464
gallery@damelioterras.com
www.damelioterras.com

STAFF

Christopher D'Amelio
Lucien Terras
Rachel Uffner
Tatiana Kronberg
Katrina Kruszewski
Denise Kupferschmidt

Noah Sheldon, **Plywood Fountain**, 2004-2005, polyurethaned birch plywood, electric pump, water, lights, rubber and bronze tubing, 48 x 48 x 16 3/4 inches; 122 x 122 x 43 cm

ARTISTS

Rob Churm
Henry Coombes
Kate Davis
Alex Frost
Charlie Hammond
Fiona Jardine
Sophie Macpherson
Alan Michael
Craig Mulholland
Alex Pollard
Gary Rough
Clare Stephenson
Michael Stumpf

ADDRESS

5-9 St Margaret's Place
G1 5JY Glasgow
SCOTLAND, UK
T: +44.1.415.532.662
F: +44.1.415.532.662
info@sorchadallas.com
www.sorchadallas.com

STAFF

Jo Charlton

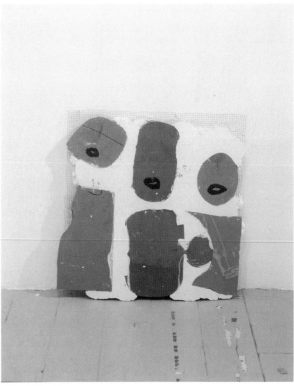

left: Alex Pollard, **Cat Monkey**, 2006, oil and enamel on bronze, 36 x 43 x 5 inches; 91 x 110 x 12 cm
right: Charlie Hammond, **Untitled (Three Ladies)**, 2005, mixed media, 23 2/3 x 22 3/4 inches; 60 x 58 cm

Thomas Dane Gallery

ARTISTS

Hurvin Anderson
José Damasceno
Anya Gallaccio
Stefan Kürten
Michael Landy
Glenn Ligon
Steve McQueen
Jean-Luc Moulène
Albert Oehlen
Paul Pfeiffer
Jorge Queiroz

ADDRESS

11 Duke Street
St. James's
SW1Y 6BN London
UNITED KINGDOM
T: +44.207.925.2505
F: +44.207.925.2506
info@thomasdane.com
www.thomasdane.com

STAFF

Thomas Dane
Martine d'Anglejan-Chatillon
François Chantala

left: Paul Pfeiffer, **Four Horsemen of the Apocalypse no. 15**, 2004, fujiflex digital c-print, edition of 6+1, 48 x 60 inches; 122 x 152.5 cm
right: Albert Oehlen, **Untitled**, 2004, oil on canvas, 86 1/2 x 106 1/4 inches; 220 x 270 cm

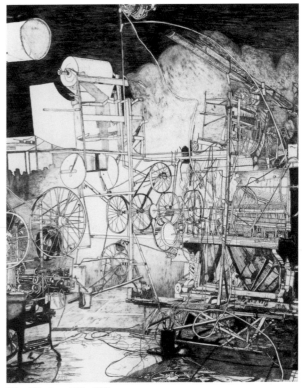

left: Michael Landy, **H.2.N.Y. Picture-making machine 2**, 2006, oil sticks on paper, 60 x 48 inches; 152 x 122 cm
right: José Damasceno, **A Gruta**, 2006, collage on photograph, series of 5, 35 1/2 x 51 1/4 inches; 90 x 130 cm

Galleria Massimo De Carlo

MILAN

ARTISTS

Amy Adler
John Armleder
Massimo Bartolini
Alighiero Boetti
Chris Burden
Maurizio Cattelan
Roberto Cuoghi
Michael Elmgreen &
   Ingar Dragset
Urs Fisher
Roland Flexner
Gelitin
Carsten Höller
Christian Holstad
Diego Perrone
Yan Pei-Ming
Paola Pivi
Ettore Spalletti

Rudolf Stingel
Piotr Uklanski
Andrea Zittel

ADDRESS

Via Giovanni Ventura, 5
I-20134 Milan
ITALY
T: +39.02.7000.3987
F: +39.02.7492.135
info@massimodecarlo.it
www.massimodecarlo.it

STAFF

Ludovica Barbieri
Manfred H. Teupen
Paola Clerico
Anna Maria Soverini
Sara Cappelletti
Elena Tavecchia

Yan Pei-Ming, **One Dollar Bill**, 2006, watercolor on paper, 60 2/3 x 91 inches; 154 x 231 cm

Deitch Projects   NEW YORK

ARTISTS

Tauba Auerbach
Kristin Baker
E.V. Day
Jim Isermann
Brad Kahlhamer
Kurt Kauper
Robert Lazzarini
Barry McGee
Ryan McGinness
Ted Mineo
Os Gemeos
Steve Powers
Clare Rojas
Swoon
Nari Ward
Kehinde Wiley

ADDRESS

76 Grand Street
New York, NY 10013
USA
T: +1.212.343.7300
F: +1.212.343.2954
info@deitch.com
www.deitch.com

18 Wooster Street
New York, NY 10013
USA

STAFF

Suzanne Geiss
Kathy Grayson
Nicola Vassell

Ryan McGinness, **installationview**, 2005, installation at Deitch Projects, variable dimensions

Dicksmith Gallery

LONDON

ARTISTS

Leonor Antunes
Joel Croxson
Benjamin Alexander Huseby
Edward Kay
Meiro Koizumi
George Henry Longly
Duncan Marquiss
Rupert Norfolk

ADDRESS

74 Buttesland Street
Hoxton
N1 6BY London
UNITED KINGDOM
T: +44.207.253.0663
info@dicksmithgallery.co.uk
www.dicksmithgallery.co.uk

STAFF

Thomas Hanbury
Rodolphe von Hofmannsthal

Edward Kay, **The Gentleman**, 2006, oil on canvas on panel, 21 x 15 inches; 53.5 x 38 cm

Galerie EIGEN + ART

BERLIN/LEIPZIG

ARTISTS

Akos Birkas
Birgit Brenner
Martin Eder
Tim Eitel
Nina Fischer/
    Maroan el Sani
Joerg Herold
Christine Hill
Uwe Kowski
Rémy Markowitsch
Maix Mayer
Carsten Nicolai
Olaf Nicolai
Neo Rauch

Ricarda Roggan
Yehudit Sasportas
David Schnell
Annelies Strba
Matthias Weischer

ADDRESS

Galerie EIGEN + ART Berlin
Auguststraße 26
D-10117 Berlin
GERMANY
T: +49.30.280.66.05
F: +49.30.280.66.16
berlin@eigen-art.com
www.eigen-art.com

Galerie EIGEN + ART Leipzig
Spinnereistraße 7, Halle 5
D-04179 Leipzig
GERMANY
T: +49.341.960.78.86
F: +49.341.225.42.14
leipzig@eigen-art.com

STAFF

Gerd Harry Lybke
Kerstin Wahala
Birte Kleemann

Jörg Herold, **"Lichtwerfer"** from the series **"Classic Fight Culture"**, 2005, B/W copies over-painted with stain, latex, watercolour, 16 1/2 x 11 5/8 inches;
42 x 29.6 cm

Ronald Feldman Fine Arts, Inc.

ARTISTS

Eleanor Antin
Ida Applebroog
Conrad Atkinson
Joseph Beuys
Alexander Brodsky
Nancy Chunn
Keith Cottingham
Milena Dopitová
Terry Fox
Carl Fudge
Rico Gatson
Leon Golub
Helen Mayer Harrison &
    Newton Harrison
Cameron Hayes
Kelly Heaton

Christine Hill
Peggy Jarrell Kaplan
Komar & Melamid
McCarren/Fine
Pepón Osorio
Panamarenko
Bruce Pearson
Jason Salavon
Edwin Schlossberg
Todd Siler
Tavares Strachan
Mierle Laderman Ukeles
Andy Warhol
Clemens Weiss
Allan Wexler
Hannah Wilke

ADDRESS

31 Mercer Street
New York, NY 10013
USA
T: +1.212.226.3232
F: +1.212.941.1536
info@feldmangallery.com
www.feldmangallery.com

STAFF

Ronald Feldman
Frayda Feldman
Martina Batan
Marco Nocella
Peggy Kaplan
Sarah H. Paulson

Tavares Strachan, **Compound Cloud (impending storm) from Cloud Chamber Series 1**, 2006, 1 of 30 photographs mounted on individual lightboxes, 12 x 9 3/4 inches; 30.5 x 24.8 cm

Keith Cottingham, still from 3D animation, 2006

Zach Feuer Gallery

NEW YORK

ARTISTS

Jules de Balincourt
Tamy Ben-Tor
Nathalie Djurberg
Luis Gispert
Daniel Gordon
Stuart Hawkins
Anton Henning
Ridley Howard
Paul Ramirez Jonas
Justin Lieberman
Tim Lokiec
Tom McGrath
Jin Meyerson
Danica Phelps
Tal R
Christoph Ruckhäberle
Dana Schutz

Simone Shubuck
Aaron Spangler
Johannes VanDerBeek
Phoebe Washburn

ADDRESS

530 West 24th Street
New York, NY 10011
USA
T: +1.212.989.7700
F: +1.212.989.7720
info@zachfeuer.com
www.zachfeuer.com

STAFF

Zach Feuer
Grace Evans
Lumi Tan
Benjamin King

Daniel Gordon, **No Title**, 2006, C-print, 14 x 11 inches; 35.6 x 27.9 cm

Marc Foxx

ARTISTS

Richard Aldrich
Ryoko Aoki
Cris Brodahl
Brian Calvin
Jay Chung
Anne Collier
Andy Collins
Martin Creed
William Daniels
Stef Driesen
Brian Fahlstrom
Vincent Fecteau
Ryan Gander
Roger Hiorns
Jim Hodges
Evan Holloway
Annette Kelm
Makiko Kudo

Luisa Lambri
Jason Meadows
Carter Mull
David Musgrave
Philippe Perrot
Alessandro Pessoli
Richard Rezac
Matthew Ronay
Sterling Ruby
Maaike Schoorel
Frances Stark
Hiroshi Sugito
Jan Timme
Nicola Tyson
Hellen van Meene
Sophie von Hellermann
Karlheinz Weinberger

ADDRESS

1650 Wilshire Boulevard
Los Angeles, CA 90048
USA
T: +1.323.857.5571
F: +1.323.857.5573
gallery@marcfoxx.com
www.marcfoxx.com

STAFF

Marc Foxx, Partner
Rodney Hill, Partner
Lia Trinka-Browner
Baker Montgomery

Roger Hiorns, **The Architect's Mother**, 2003, copper sulfate, BMW engine, steel, cardboard, foam, 91 x 51 x 34 inches; 231 x 130 x 86 cm
Installation view Hammer Museum

Foxy Production

NEW YORK

ARTISTS	ADDRESS	STAFF
Jimmy Baker	617 West 27 Street	Michael Gillespie,
Michael Bell-Smith	Ground Floor	Owner/Director
Violet Hopkins	New York, NY 10001	John Thomson,
Paper Rad	USA	Owner/Director
Ester Partegàs	T: +1.212.239.2758	Chelsea Goodchild,
David Noonan	F: +1.212.239.2759	Registrar
Sterling Ruby	info@foxyproduction.com	
Yuh-Shioh Wong	www.foxyproduction.com	

David Noonan, **Untitled**, 2006, paper collage, 10 x 8 inches; 25.4 x 20.32 cm

Fredericks & Freiser

NEW YORK

ARTISTS

Linda Burnham
Justin Craun
Nicholas Di Genova
Jeff Elrod
Steve Gianakos
Zeng Hao
Sean McCarthy
Julie Moos
Estate of Robert Overby
Baker Overstreet
Lamar Peterson
Zak Smith
Max Toth
Thomas Trosch
Marnie Weber
John Wesley

ADDRESS

536 West 24th Street
New York, NY 10011
USA
T: +1.212.633.6555
F: +1.212.633.7372
info@fredericksfreiser
   gallery.com
www.fredericksfreiser
   gallery.com

STAFF

Jessica Fredericks
Andrew Freiser
Monica Ramos
Lizzie Stein

Baker Overstreet, **Broadwaylegz**, 2006, oil on canvas, 84 x 72 inches; 213 x 183 cm

Frith Street Gallery

LONDON

ARTISTS

Chantal Akerman
Polly Apfelbaum
Fiona Banner
Anna Barriball
Massimo Bartolini
Dorothy Cross
Tacita Dean
Marlene Dumas
Craigie Horsfield
Callum Innes
Jaki Irvine
Cornelia Parker
Giuseppe Penone
John Riddy
Thomas Schütte
Dayanita Singh

Bridget Smith
Annelies Strba
Fiona Tan
Juan Uslé
Daphne Wright

ADDRESS

59-60 Frith Street
W1D 3JJ London
UNITED KINGDOM
T: +44.207.494.1550
F: +44.207.287.3733
info@frithstreetgallery.com
www.frithstreetgallery.com

STAFF

Jane Hamlyn
Charlotte Schepke

Fiona Banner, **Tornado Nude,** 2006 (Installation View), Tornado Airplane Wing, paint, 232 1/4 x 90 2/3 x 110 1/6 inches; 590 x 230 x 280 cm

Galerist   ISTANBUL

ARTISTS

Haluk Akakce
Taner Ceylan
Guillermo Calzadilla
Hussein Chalayan
Ayse Erkmen
Leyla Gediz
Yesim Akdeniz Graf
Serkan Ozkaya
Guclu Oztekin
Seza Paker
Erinc Seymen
Murat Sahinler
Evren Tekinoktay
Elif Uras

ADDRESS

Istiklal cad. Misir art.
311/4 Beyoglu
34340 Istanbul
TURKEY
T: +90.212.244.8230
F: +90.212.244.8229
info@galerist.com.tr
www.galerist.com.tr

STAFF

Murat Pilevneli
Lori Sardinas
Ebru Algim
Burcu Gokcek

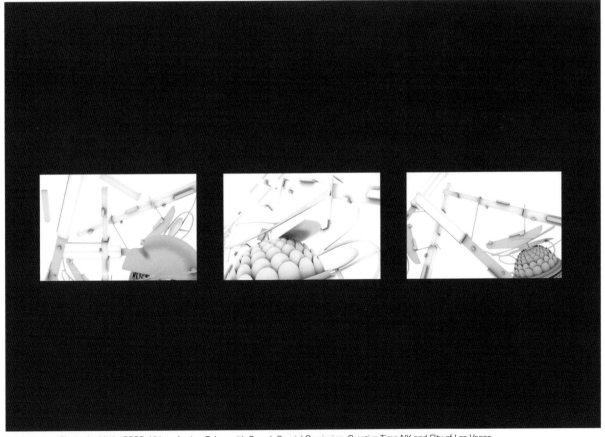

Haluk Akakce, **Sky is the Limit**, 2006, Video, 4 min., Colour with Sound, Special Comission, Creative Time NY and City of Las Vegas

Gavlak

ARTISTS

Jose Alvarez
Lisa Anne Auerbach
Andisheh Avini
Carolyn Carr
Bettina Brüning
Phillip Estlund
Wade Guyton
Sandra Hamburg
Anthony James
Kathleen Johnson
Miyeon Lee
Marilyn Minter
Aleksandra Mir
Aleksandra Penney
Alexis Marguerite Teplin
Elif Uras
TJ Wilcox

ADDRESS

3300 South Dixie Highway
Suite 4
West Palm Beach
FL 33405
USA
T: +1.561.833.0583
F: +1.561.214.4526
info@gavlakprojects.com
www.gavlakprojects.com

STAFF

Sarah Gavlak
Cristin Lane

Alexis Marguerite Teplin, **L'Robe a Ramages 1891**, 2004-05, oil on canvas, 85 x 61 inches; 216 x 155 cm

Annet Gelink Gallery

ARTISTS

Rita Ackermann
Carlos Amorales
Armando Andrade Tudela
Yael Bartana
Delphine Courtillot
Ed van der Elsken
Alicia Framis
Anya Gallaccio
Ryan Gander
Carla Klein
Kiki Lamers
David Maljković
Victor Man
Jenny Perlin
Liza May Post

Muzi Quawson
Glenn Sorensen
Barbara Visser
Erik Wesselo
Floor Wullems

ADDRESS

Laurierstraat 187-189
NL-1016PL Amsterdam
THE NETHERLANDS
T: +31.20.330.20.66
F: +31.20.330.20.65
info@annetgelink.com
www.annetgelink.com

STAFF

Annet Gelink, Director
Annelieke van Halen
Martijn van den Bosch

Ryan Gander, **A Slowing of the Spectator's Eye**, 2005, fibreglass wall, 118 x 236 1/6 inches; 300 x 600 cm

GERING & LóPEZ GALLERY

NEW YORK

ARTISTS

Hannah Collins
Peter Halley
José-Antonio Hernández Díez
Craig Kauffman
Alix Lambert
Matthew McCaslin
Igor Mischiyev
John F. Simon Jr.
Jane Simpson
Xavier Veilhan
Leo Villareal
José Ma Yturralde

ADDRESS

730 Fifth Avenue
New York, NY 10019
USA
T: +1.646.336.7183
F: +1.646.336.7185
info@geringlopez.com
www.geringlopez.com

STAFF

Sandra Gering
Javier López
Karen LaGatta, Director
Russell Calabrese,
    Associate
Lauren Cicione, Associate

Matthew McCaslin, **Endless Meditation**, 2006, 32" flat screen TV, DVD player, fluorescent light fixtures with black light bulbs and packing peanuts

Greenberg Van Doren Gallery

NEW YORK

ARTISTS

Emi Avora
Katherine Bowling
James Brooks
Suzanne Caporael
Jessica Craig-Martin
Tim Davis
Richard Diebenkorn
Benjamin Edwards
Sharon Ellis
Paul Graham
Katy Grannan
Julia Kunin
Eva Lundsager
Elizabeth Magill
Malerie Mardner
Cameron Martin
Barry Ratoff
Dorothea Rockburne

Aïda Ruilova
Alexis Smith
Lane Twitchell
Kevin Zucker

ADDRESS

730 Fifth Avenue, 7th Floor
New York, NY 10019
USA
T: +1.212.445.0444
F: +1.212.445.0442
info@gvdgallery.com
www.gvdgallery.com

STAFF

Dorsey Waxter, Director
Elizabeth Raizes,
    Associate Director
Augusto Arbizo, Curator
Georgia Franklin,
    Associate Director
Paul Brainard, Preparator
Jane Parshall, Archivist

Katy Grannan, **Gail, Baker Beach (diptych)**, 2005 , C-print, edition of 6, 28 1/2 x 35 1/8 inches each; 72 x 89 cm

Greene Naftali

NEW YORK

ARTISTS

Julie Becker
Paul Chan
Tony Conrad
Jim Drain
Harun Farocki
Lucy Gunning
Guyton \ Walker
Rachel Harrison
Richard Hawkins
Jacqueline Humphries
Joachim Koester
David Korty
Michael Krebber
Michaela Meise
Mai-Thu Perret
Daniel Pflumm

Daniela Rossell
Josef Strau
Sophie von Hellermann
Katharina Wulff
Amelie von Wulffen

ADDRESS

508 West 26th Street
8th Floor
New York, NY 10001
USA
T: +1.212.463.7770
F: +1.212.463.0890
info@greenenaftali
   gallery.com
www.greenenaftali
   gallery.com

STAFF

Carol Greene
Jay Sanders
Alexandra Tuttle

Paul Chan, **1st Light**, 2005, digital video projection, 14:00

greengrassi   LONDON

ARTISTS

Tomma Abts
Jennifer Bornstein
Roe Ethridge
Gretchen Faust
Giuseppe Gabellone
Ellen Gronemeyer
Margherita Manzelli
Aleksandra Mir
David Musgrave
Silke Otto-Knapp
Alessandro Pessoli
Karin Ruggaber
Anne Ryan
Frances Stark
Pae White
Lisa Yuskavage

ADDRESS

1a Kempsford Road
(off Wincott Street)
SE11 4NU London
UNITED KINGDOM
T: +44.20.7840.9101
F: +44.20.7840.9102
info@greengrassi.com
www.greengrassi.com

STAFF

Cornelia Grassi
Megan O'Shea
Lindsay Jarvis

Giuseppe Gabellone, **Untitled**, 2006, mirrored glass on wood, 102 3/8 x 63 x 63 inches; 260 x 160 x 160 cm

Galeria Enrique Guerrero

MEXICO

ARTISTS

Rubén Gutiérrez
Pablo Helguera
Enrique Jezik
Yoshua Okon
Quirarte & Ornelas
Ricardo Rendón
Richard Stipl
Luis Miguel Suro

ADDRESS

Horacio 1549-A
Col. Polanco CP
Mexico DF 11540
MEXICO
T: +52.55.5280.2941/
  5183
F: +52.55.5280.5283
info@galeriaenriqueguerrero
  .com
www.galeriaenriqueguerrero
  .com

STAFF

Enrique Guerrero
Fernanda Rangel
Rebeca Rodríguez
Javier Nieves
Marco Alcantar

Enrique Jezik, **Practica (50 cartridges caliber 12)**, 2006, Ten shooting practice silhouettes on wood each one with five shotguns, Variable measures

Jack Hanley Gallery

SAN FRANCISCO

ARTISTS

Carter
Anne Collier
Simon Evans
Harrell Fletcher
Christopher Garrett
David Godbold
Piotr Janas
Jo Jackson
Chris Johanson
Jim Lambie
Saskia Leek
Ed Loftus
Camilla Low
Euan MacDonald
Andrew Mania
Alicia McCarthy
Adam McEwen
Keegan McHargue
Jonathon Monk

Muntean/Rosenblum
Scott Myles
Shaun O'Dell
Bill Owens
Will Rogan
Scott Reeder
Tyson Reeder
Michael Sailstorfer
Leslie Shows
Hayley Tompkins
Donald Urquhart
Anna VonMertens
Chris Ware
Erwin Wurm

ADDRESS

395 Valencia Street
San Francisco, CA 94103
USA
T: +1.415.522.1623
F: +1.415.522.1631
info@jackhanley.com
www.jackhanley.com

945 Sun Mun Way
Los Angeles, CA 90012
T: +1.213.626.0403

STAFF

Jack Hanley, Director
Alexandra Gaty
Ava Jancar
Dina Pugh

Keegan McHargue, **Untitled (White Male...)**, 2006, acrylic on panel, 40 x 50 inches; 102 x 127 cm

Harris Lieberman

ARTISTS

Stef Driesen
Daniel Guzmán
Karl Haendel
Evan Holloway
Yasue Maetake
Ohad Meromi
Rosalind Nashashibi
Michael Queenland
Matt Saunders
Tommy White
Aaron Young
Thomas Zipp

ADDRESS

89 Vandam Street
New York, NY 10013
USA
T: +1.212.206.1290
F: +1.212.604.0203
gallery@harrislieberman
   .com
www.harrislieberman.com

STAFF

Jessie Washburne-Harris
Michael Lieberman
Allison Kave

Matt Saunders, **Matti Pellonpää (Lobby Cards)**, 2006 (detail), 12 black and white photographs (contact prints) from hand-drawn negatives,
9 1/4 x 11 1/4 inches each; 24 x 29 cm, Edition of 2

ARTISTS

Haluk Akakçe
Phillip Allen
Cris Brodahl
Patrick Hill
Evan Holloway
Inventory
Germaine Kruip
Rezi van Lankveld
Dave Muller
Jacques Nimki
Michael Raedecker
Brett Cody Rogers
John Stezaker

Mari Sunna
Evren Tekinoktay
Gary Webb
Martin Westwood
Tom Wood
Shizuka Yokomizo

ADDRESS

6 Haunch of Venison Yard
off Brook Street
W1K 5ES London
UNITED KINGDOM
T: +44.207.495.5050
F: +44.207.495.4050
london@haunchof
   venison.com
www.haunchofvenison.com

Lessingstrasse 5
CH-8002 Zurich
SWITZERLAND
T: +41.43.422.8888
F: +41.43.422.8889
zurich@haunchofveni
   son.com

STAFF

Harry Blain, Director
Pilar Corrias, Director
Juerg Judin, Director,
Graham Southern, Director
Adrian Sutton, Director

Patrick Tuttofuoco, **On the corner where we stand (Shanghai)**, 2006, Steel, mirror, plastic, adhesive pvc, 53 x 53 x 137 3/4 inches; 135 x 135 x 350 cm

Hauser & Wirth Zürich London

ARTISTS

Louise Bourgeois
Christoph Büchel
David Claerbout
Martin Creed
Berlinde De Bruyckere
Ellen Gallagher
Isa Genzken
Dan Graham
Rodney Graham
David Hammons
Mary Heilmann
The Estate of Eva Hesse
Andreas Hofer
Roni Horn
Richard Jackson
Allan Kaprow
On Kawara
Rachel Khedoori
Guillermo Kuitca
Maria Lassnig

The Estate of Lee Lozano
Paul McCarthy
John McCracken
Caro Niederer
Christopher Orr
Raymond Pettibon
Michael Raedecker
Jason Rhoades
Pipilotti Rist
Anri Sala
Wilhelm Sasnal
Christoph Schlingensief
Roman Signer
Tony Smith
Diana Thater
André Thomkins
Zhang Enli
David Zink Yi
Jakub Julian Ziolkowski

ADDRESS

Limmatstrasse 270
CH-8031 Zürich
SWITZERLAND
T: +41.44.446.8050
F: +41.44.446.8055
zurich@hauserwirth.com
www.hauserwirth.com

196A Piccadilly
London W1J 9DY
Tel. +44.207.287.23.00
Fax +44.207.287.66.00
london@hauserwirth.com
www.hauserwirth.com

STAFF

Iwan Wirth, President
Marc Payot, Partner
Florian Berktold, Director
Gregor Muir, Director
Cornelia Providoli, Director

Christoph Büchel, **Hole**, 2005, Installation (Installation view Kunsthalle Basel), Dimensions variable

ARTISTS	ADDRESS	STAFF
Jessica Bronson	2766 S. La Cienega Blvd	Anna Helwing
Henry Coombes	Los Angeles, CA 90034	Stacy Fertig
Karl Haendel	USA	Morgan Satterfield
Emilie Halpern	T: +310.202.2213	
Skylar Haskard	F: +310.202.2214	
Lutz/Guggisberg	info@annahelwing	
Kelly Poe	gallery.com	
Robert Russell	www.annahelwing	
Maya Schindler	gallery.com	
Mindy Shapero		
Mario Ybarra Jr.		

Karl Haendel, **Headlines #1**, 2006, pencil on paper, 45 x 70 inches; 114 x 178 cm

Herald St

LONDON

ARTISTS	ADDRESS	STAFF
Markus Amm	2 Herald St	Nicky Verber
Alexandra Bircken	E2 6JT London	Ash Lange
Pablo Bronstein	UNITED KINGDOM	
Spartacus Chetwynd	T: +44.20.7168.2566	
Peter Coffin	F: +44.20.7168.2566	
Scott King	mail@heraldst.com	
Cary Kwok	www.heraldst.com	
Christina Mackie		
Djordje Ozbolt		
Oliver Payne & Nick Relph		
Tony Swain		
Donald Urquhart		
Klaus Weber		
Nicole Wermers		

Donald Urquhart, **Last Night**, 2006, ink on paper, 16 1/2 x 11 3/4 inches; 42 x 29.7 cm

ARTISTS	ADDRESS	STAFF
Rita Ackermann	53 Old Bethnal Green Road	Darren Flook
Michael Bauer	E2 6QA London	Christabel Stewart
Carol Bove	UNITED KINGDOM	Margherita Hohenlohe
Carter	T: +44.20.7729 3122	
Steven Claydon	F: +44.20.7739.4095	
Luke Dowd	email@generalhotel.org	
Richard Kern	www.generalhotel.org	
Alastair MacKinven		
Alan Michael		
David Noonan		
Peter Saville		
Torsten Slama		
Alexis Marguerite Teplin		

Alastair MacKinven, **Massa Peel**, 2006, framed found photograph with text, 15 3/8 x 15 inches; 39 x 38.2 cm (framed)

Daniel Hug   LOS ANGELES

ARTISTS

Patterson Beckwith
Hanna-Mari Blencke
Gaylen Gerber
Dave Hullfish Bailey
Ulrich Lamsfuss
Eli Langer
Chris Lipomi
T. Kelly Mason
Florian Morlat
Michael Queenland
Markus Selg
Stephanie Taylor
Michael Wilkinson
Thomas Zipp

ADDRESS

510 Bernard Street
Los Angeles, CA 90012
USA
T: +1.323.221.0016
F: +1.323.343.1133
gallery@danielhug.com
www.danielhug.com

STAFF

Daniel Hug

Michael Wilkinson, **Wall**, 2005, etched mirror, wood, enamel paint, 96 1/10 x 62 1/5 x 1 3/5 inches; 244 x 158 x 4 cm

IBID PROJECTS

LONDON

ARTISTS

Jānis Avotins
Guillermo Caivano
Ross Chisholm
Anthea Hamilton
William Hunt
Christopher Orr
Anj Smith
Nedko Solakov

ADDRESS

21 Vyner Street
E2 9DG London
UNITED KINGDOM
T: +44.208.983.4355
F: +44.208.980.4605
info@ibidprojects.com
www.ibidprojects.com

STAFF

Vita Zaman, Director
Magnus Edensvard,
   Director
Tobias Wagner,
   Assistant Director
Romilly Eveleigh,
   Gallery Manager

Anj Smith, **Miasma**, 2006, oil on linen, 8 x 10 inches; 20.5 x 25.5 cm

in Situ

PARIS

ARTISTS	**ADDRESS**	**STAFF**
Andrea Blum	10, rue Duchefdelaville	Fabienne Leclerc
Lynne Cohen	F-75013 Paris	Rebecca Fanuele
Patrick Corillon	FRANCE	Camille Courtinat
Damien Deroubaix	T: +33.1.53.79.06.12	
Mark Dion	F: +33.1.53.79.06.19	
Harrell Fletcher	fabienne.leclerc@wana	
Subodh Gupta	doo.fr	
Gary Hill	www.insituparis.fr	
Noritoshi Hirakawa		
Los Carpinteros		
Florence Paradeis		
Bruno Perramant		
The Blue Noses		
Laurent Tixador & Abraham		
Poincheval		
Patrick van Caeckenbergh		

left: Subodh Gupta, **The Way Home I**, 1998-99, stainless steel, fibreglass object, dimensions variable
right: Damien Deroubaix, **Revelations**, 2006, watercolor, ink, acrylic, collage and engraving on wood on paper, 129 9/10 x 177 1/5 inches; 330 x 450 cm

Taka Ishii Gallery   TOKYO

ARTISTS

Amy Adler
Doug Aitken
Nobuyoshi Araki
Slater Bradley
Jeff Burton
Thomas Demand
Jason Dodge
Elmgreen & Dragset
Kevin Hanley
Naoya Hatakeyama
Tomoki Imai
Naoto Kawahara
Yuki Kimura
Sean Landers
Daido Moriyama
Kyoko Murase
Silke Otto-Knapp
Jorge Pardo

Erik Parker
Jack Pierson
Hiroe Saeki
Dean Sameshima
Kei Takemura
Kara Walker
Chirstopher Wool

ADDRESS

1-3-2 5F Kiyosumi Koto-ku
135-0024 Tokyo
JAPAN
T: +81.3.5646.6050
F: +81.3.3642.3067
tig@takaishiigallery.com
www.takaishiigallery.com

STAFF

Takayuki Ishii,
   Owner/Director
Jeffrey Ian Rosen, Director
Elisa Uematsu, Director
Nahoko Yamaguchi,
   Director

Kei Takemura, **rolling with dearest You**, 2006, bed used by k.t., used Ikea bed, used south German country style bed, German country style bed, wood, used cloth by K.T., K.T., H.T., Y.K., M.F., A.T., A.T.'s boyfriend D., Y.S., F.S., C.S., R.F., T.N., S.H.,S.H.'s girlfriend, S.H., K.K., K.K.'s brother, S.M., A.S., F.K., S.K., K.M., K.M.'s known baby, Y.K., A.T., M.F., A.F., drawing, wood, metal pole, and metal fittings, 52 1/5 x 123 1/5 x 141 7/10 inches; 130 x 313 x 360 cm

Alison Jacques Gallery
LONDON

ARTISTS

Uta Barth
Liz Craft
Tomory Dodge
Stef Driesen
Christian Flamm
Mark Flores
Ian Kiaer
Graham Little
Robert Mapplethorpe
Paul Morrison
Jack Pierson
Jon Pylypchuk
Alessandro Raho
Sam Salisbury
Michael Van Ofen
Catherine Yass
Thomas Zipp

ADDRESS

4 Clifford Street
W1X 1RB London
UNITED KINGDOM
T: +44.20.728.77675
F: +44.20.728.77674
info@alisonjacques
    gallery.com
www.alisonjacques
    gallery.com

STAFF

Alison Jacques
Tim Warner-Johnson
Laura Lord

Catherine Yass, **Lock (open)**, 2006, Ilfochrome transparency, lightbox, 40 1/8 x 51 1/8 x 6 1/2 inches; 102 x 130 x 16.5 cm

Johnen/Schöttle

ARTISTS

Janis Avotins
Stephan Balkenhol
Roger Ballen
Armin Boehm
Martin Boyce
Michal Budny
Rafal Bujnowski
David Claerbout
James Coleman
Martin Creed
Slawomir Elsner
Elger Esser
Hans-Peter Feldmann
Francesco Gennari
Dan Graham
Rodney Graham
Stefan Hablützel
Thomas Helbig
Uwe Henneken
Candida Höfer
Martin Honert

Olaf Holzapfel
Jakub Hosek
Robert Kusmirowski
Marcin Lukasiewicz
Mindaugas Lukosaitis
Victor Man
Jan Merta
Yoshitomo Nara
Djordje Ozbolt
Pietro Roccasalva
Thomas Ruff
Anri Sala
Wilhelm Sasnal
Tino Sehgal
Helmut Stallaerts
Thomas Struth
Florian Süßmayr
Jeff Wall
Jakub Julian Ziolkowski
Thomas Zipp

ADDRESS

Maria-Hilf-Strasse 17
D-50677 Cologne
GERMANY
T: +49.221.310.270
F: +49.221.310.2727
mail@johnen-schoettle.de
www.johnen-schoettle.de

Schillingstrasse 31
D-10179 Berlin
GERMANY
T: +49.30.2758.3030
F: +49.30.2758.3050
mail@johnengalerie.de
www.johnengalerie.de

Amalienstrasse 41
D-80799 Munich
T: +49.89.333.686
F: +49.89.342 296
info@galerie-schoettle.de
www.galerie-ruediger-
    schoettle.de

STAFF

Jörg Johnen
Rüdiger Schöttle
Markus Lüttgen
Tan Morben
Ingrid Lohaus

Candida Hofer, **Opera Lisbon**, 2006, C-print, 80 3/4 x 99 3/8 inches; 205 x 252.6 cm

Casey Kaplan

NEW YORK

ARTISTS

Jeff Burton
Nathan Carter
Miles Coolidge
Jason Dodge
Trisha Donnelly
Pamela Fraser
Liam Gillick
Annika von Hausswolff
Carsten Höller
Brian Jungen
Jonthan Monk
Diego Perrone
Julia Schmidt
Simon Starling
Johannes Wohnseifer
Gabriel Vormstein

ADDRESS

525 West 21st Street
New York, NY 10011
USA
T: +1.212.645.7335
F: +1.212.645.7835
info@caseykaplan
  gallery.com
www.caseykaplangallery.com

STAFF

Casey Kaplan, Director
Chana Budgazad,
  Associate Director
Joanna Kleinberg, Registrar
Loring Randolph,
  Gallery Assistant

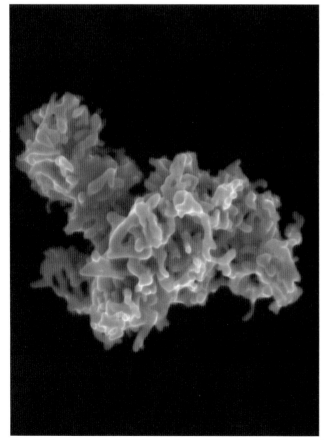

Simon Starling, **Inventar-Nr. 8573 (Man Ray)**, **4m - 400nm**, (detail), 2006, 80 6 x 7cm black and white transparencies, 2x Gotschmann Slide Projectors, Kodak Dissolve Control Unit, CD and Player Duration 8mins.

Georg Kargl

VIENNA

ARTISTS

Richard Artschwager
Clegg & Guttmann
Mark Dion
Carol Bove
Martin Dammann
Cerith Wyn Evans
Angus Fairhurst
Jitka Hanzlová
Herbert Hinteregger
Chris Johanson
Elke Krystufek
Thomas Locher
Matt Mullican
Muntean/Rosenblum
Gerwald Rockenschaub

Lisa Ruyter
Markus Schinwald
Rudolf Stingel
Gabi Trinkaus
Rosemarie Trockel
John Waters

ADDRESS

Schleifmühlgasse 5
A-1040 Vienna
AUSTRIA
T: +43.1.585.41.99
F: +43.1.585.41.999
office@georgkargl.com
www.georgkargl.com

STAFF

Georg Kargl
Pilar Alcalá
Evelyn Appinger
Fiona Liewehr

Franz Graf, **LOVEMYDREAMS**, installation view Georg Kargl Fine Arts, Vienna, 11/11/2005-14/01/2006

Galleri Magnus Karlsson

ARTISTS

Mamma Andersson
Roger Andersson
Lars Arrhenius
Bianca Maria Barmen
Amy Bennett
Mette Björnberg
Thomas Broomé
Marcel Dzama
Niklas Eneblom
Jens Fänge
Carl Hammoud
Tommy Hilding
Kent Iwemyr
Richard Johansson
Johanna Karlsson
Klara Kristalova
Petra Lindholm
Ulf Lundin

Anne-Marie Nordin
Jockum Nordström
Susanne Simonson
Anna Strid
Per Wennerstrand

ADDRESS

Fredsgatan 12
S-11152 Stockholm
SWEDEN
T: +46.8.660.43.53
info@gallerimagnus
    karlsson.com
www.gallerimagnus
    karlsson.com

STAFF

Magnus Karlsson,
    Owner/Director
Sofie Proos, Assistant
Carolina Wikström,
    Assistant

Niklas Eneblom, **My Dead Friend's Dead Friend**, 2006, Oil on canvas, 28 x 41 inches; 72 x 105 cm

Tommy Hilding, **BORDERS**, 2005, oil on linen, 71 x 53 inches; 180 x 135 cm

Paul Kasmin Gallery

NEW YORK

ARTISTS

Christopher Bucklow
Susan Derges
Angus Fairhurst
Barry Flanagan
Caio Fonseca
Walton Ford
David Hockney
Robert Indiana
Mark Innerst
Deborah Kass
Claude and Francois-Xavier
    Lalanne
Morris Louis
Santi Moix
James Nares
Jules Olitski
Elliott Puckette
Nancy Rubins

Kenny Scharf
Frank Stella
Andy Warhol
Xu Bing
Joe Zucker

ADDRESS

293 Tenth Avenue
New York, NY 10001

511 West 27th Street,
New York, NY 10001

T: +212.563.4474
F: +212.563.4494
inquiry@paulkasmingallery.com
www.paulkasmingallery.com

STAFF

Paul Kasmin
Clara Ha, Director

Deborah Kass, **Hard To Be A Jew**, 2003, oil and acrylic on canvas, 72 x 96 inches; 182.9 x 243.8 cm

Galleria Francesca Kaufmann   MILAN

ARTISTS

Candice Breitz
Pierpaolo Campanini
Gianni Caravaggio
Maggie Cardelùs
Edi Hila
Kori Newkirk
Kelly Nipper
Tam Ochiai
Yoshua Okon
Adrian Paci
Eva Rothschild
Aida Ruilova
Roberta Silva
Lily van der Stokker
Billy Sullivan
Pae White

ADDRESS

Via dell'Orso 16
I-20121 Milano
ITALY
T: +39.02.72094331
F: +39.02.72096873
info@galleriafrancesca
   kaufmann.com
www.galleriafrancesca
   kaufmann.com

STAFF

Francesca Kaufmann
Alessio delli Castelli
Chiara Repetto
Livia Fallarino

Adrian Paci, **Per Speculum**, 2006, printed photograph, 31 1/2 x 43 1/6 inches; 80 x 120 cm

Sean Kelly Gallery

NEW YORK

ARTISTS

Marina Abramovic
Laurie Anderson
Christine Borland
Los Carpinteros
James Casebere
Helmut Dorner
Iran do Espírito Santo
Antony Gormley
Johan Grimonprez
Ann Hamilton
Rebecca Horn
Callum Innes
Ilya & Emilia Kabakov
Estate of Seydou Keïta
Joseph Kosuth
Robert Mapplethorpe
Anthony McCall

Julie Roberts
Julião Sarmento
Lorna Simpson
Pia Stadtbäumer
Frank Thiel
Gavin Turk

ADDRESS

528 West 29th Street
New York, NY 10001
USA
T: +1.212.239.1181
F: +1.212.239.2467
info@skny.com
www.skny.com

STAFF

Sean Kelly
Cecile Panzieri,
    Executive Director
Denis Gardarin, Director
Boshko Boskovic,
    Associate Director

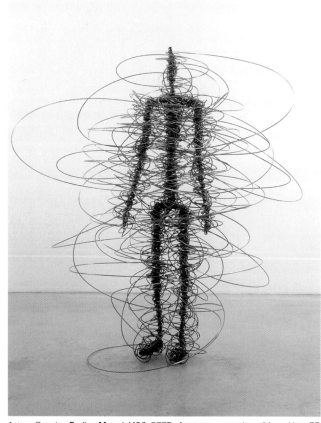

Antony Gormley, **Feeling Material XVI**, 2005, 4mm square section mild steel bar, 77 1/2 x 73 x 51 inches; 197 x 186 x 130cm

ARTISTS

Phillip Allen
Phil Collins
Dorothy Cross
Willie Doherty
Mark Francis
Maureen Gallace
David Godbold
Siobhan Hapaska
Callum Innes
Jaki Irvine
Merlin James
Elizabeth Magill
Stephen McKenna
William McKeown
Isabel Nolan
Kathy Prendergast

Norbert Schwontkowski
Paul Seawright
Tony Swain
Paul Winstanley

ADDRESS

Anne's Lane
South Anne Street
D2 Dublin
IRELAND
T: +353.1.670903
F: + 353.670906
gallery@kerlin.ie
www.kerlin.ie

STAFF

David Fitzgerald
Darrag Hogan
John Kennedy

Kathy Prendergast , **Big Universe**, 2006, painted bronze, unique, 12.6 x 9.4 x 7.9 inches; 32 x 24 x 20 cm

Anton Kern Gallery

NEW YORK

ARTISTS

Nobuyoshi Araki
Ellen Berkenblit
John Bock
Brian Calvin
Saul Fletcher
Mark Grotjahn
Bendix Harms
Eberhard Havekost
Lothar Hempel
Jörg Immendorff
Sergej Jensen
Sarah Jones
Michael Joo
Edward Krasinski
Jim Lambie
Marepe
Dan McCarthy
Enrique Metinides

Matthew Monahan
Marcel Odenbach
Manfred Pernice
Alessandro Pessoli
Wilhelm Sasnal
Lara Schnitger
David Shrigley
Andy Warhol

ADDRESS

532 West 20th Streeet
New York, NY 10011
USA
T: +1.212.367.9663
F: +1.212.367.8135
info@antonkerngallery.com
www.antonkerngallery.com

STAFF

Anton Kern
Michael Clifton
Christoph Gerozissis
Jeffrey Porterfield
Emily Schroeder
Joshua Smith

Jim Lambie, installation view at Anton Kern Gallery, New York 2006

ARTISTS	ADDRESS	STAFF
Ryoko Aoki	4-2-10 Bingomachi Chuo-ku	Kimiyoshi Kodama,
Olaf Breuning	541-0051 Osaka	Director
Masanori Handa	JAPAN	Ken Kobayashi
Zon Ito	T: +81.6.4707.8872	Yutaka Taniguchi
Tomoki Kakitani	F: +81.6.4707.8873	Sakura Shimizu
Teppei Kaneuji	info@KodamaGallery.com	
Yuki Kimura	www.KodamaGallery.com	
Chihiro Mori		
Torawo Nakagawa	3-7-4F Nishigokencho	
Daisuke Nakayama	Shinjuku-ku	
Katsushige Nakahashi	162-0812 Tokyo	
Minako Nishiyama	JAPAN	
Torbjørn Rødland	T: +81.3.5261.9022	
Una Szeemann	F: +81.3.5225.7063	
Tadasu Takamine		
Hidekazu Tanaka		

Chihiro Mori, **0 kHz / KOMUSOU** civilization, charcoal, felt-tip pen on Japanese paper mounted on wood panel / clay sculpture, wooden object, brush, gaine, 2005, 63 x 63 inches; 160 x 160 cm; 52 3/4 x 19 3/4 x 19 3/4 inches; 50 x 50 x 134(h) cm

Leo Koenig, Inc.

ARTISTS

Aidas Bareikis
Norbert Bisky
Greg Bogin
Nicole Eisenman
Justin Faunce
Torben Giehler
Brandon Lattu
Marcin Maciejowski
Tony Matelli
Jonathan Meese
Bjarne Melgaard
Erik Parker
Alexis Rockman
Les Rogers

Tom Sanford
David Scher
Christian Schumann
Kelli WIlliams

ADDRESS

545 West 23rd Street
New York, NY 10011
USA
T: +1.212.334.9255
F: +1.212.334.9304
info@leokoenig.com
www.leokoenig.com

STAFF

Elizabeth Balogh, Director
Kai Heinze, Director
Anila Churi, Assistant
Shella Robinson, Assistant

Gelitin, **Tantamounter**, Installation View, November 2005

ARTISTS	ADDRESS	STAFF
Micol Assaël	Dessauer Strasse 6-7	Johann König
Manuel Graf	D-10963 Berlin	Kirsa Geiser
Tue Greenfort	GERMANY	
Jeppe Hein	T: +49.30.2610.3080	
Annette Kelm	F: +49.30.2610.30811	
Lisa Lapinski	info@johannkoenig.de	
Kris Martin	www.johannkoenig.de	
Michaela Meise		
Natascha Sadr Haghighian		
Michael Sailstorfer		
Johannes Wohnseifer		
Jordan Wolfson		
David Zink Yi		
Andreas Zybach		

Tue Greenfort, **Artificial Tree**, 2005, photography, 8 3/4 x 6 1/3 inches; 22 x 16 cm

David Kordansky Gallery

LOS ANGELES

ARTISTS

Markus Amm
Amy Bessone
Matthew Brannon
Samara Caughey
Steven Claydon
Aaron Curry
Sean Dack
Mark Flores
Will Fowler
Patrick Hill
Violet Hopkins
Thomas Houseago
William Jones
Alan Michael

David Noonan
Brett Cody Rogers
Lesley Vance
Nicolau Vergueiro

ADDRESS

510 Bernard Street
Los Angeles, CA 90012
USA
T: +1.323.222.1482
F: +1.323.227.7933
info@davidkordansky
    gallery.com
www.davidkordansky
    gallery.com

STAFF

David Kordansky
Natasha Garcia-Lomas,
    Director
Joel Holmberg,
    Associate Director

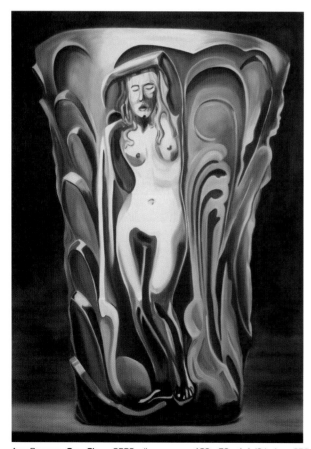

Amy Bessone, **Gray Glass**, 2006, oil on canvas , 102 x 72 x 1 1/2 inches; 259.1 x 182.9 x 3.8 cm

ARTISTS	ADDRESS	STAFF

Satoshi Ohno

1-3-2-7F Kiyosumi
Koto-ku
135-0024 Tokyo
JAPAN
T: +81.3.3642.4090
F: +81.3.3642.4091
info@tomiokoyama
  gallery.com
www.tomiokoyama
  gallery.com

Tomio Koyama, Owner
Yuko Nagase, Director
Daisuke Watanabe
Kosaku Kanechika
Tomoko Omori
Namie Kuwada
Kaoru Chiba
Takeshi Abe

Satoshi Ohno, **acid garden**, 2006, mixed media

Andrew Kreps Gallery

NEW YORK

ARTISTS

Ricci Albenda
Daniel Bozhkov
Peter Coffin
Roe Ethridge
Jonah Freeman
Uwe Henneken
Jamie Isenstein
Ján Mančuška
Robert Melee
Peter Piller
Ruth Root
Lawrence Seward
Padraig Timoney
Cheyney Thompson
Hayley Tompkins
Klaus Weber

ADDRESS

525 West 22nd Street
New York, NY 10011
USA
T: +1.212.741.8849
F: +1.212.741.8163
contact@andrewkreps.com
www.andrewkreps.com

STAFF

Andrew Kreps
Liz Mulholland
Ezra Rubin
Erin Somerville

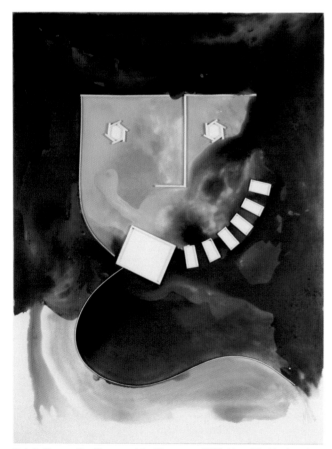

Padraig Timoney, **The Shaves and the Shave-nots**, 2005, Ink, rabbit skin glue, pigment, and wood on canvas , 47 1/4 x 35 1/2 inches; 120 x 90.2 cm

Galerie Krinzinger

VIENNA

ARTISTS

Atelier van Lieshout
Chris Burden
Günter Brus
Angela de la Cruz
Dubossarsky & Vinogradov
Ann-Kristin Hamm
Ken Kagami
Zenita Komad
Valery Koshlyakov
Angelika Krinzinger
Erik van Lieshout
Jonathan Meese
Bjarne Melgaard
Shintaro Miyake

Alois Mosbacher
Otto Muehl
Hermann Nitsch
Hans Op de Beeck
Sigmar Polke
Werner Reiterer
Eva Schlegel
Rudolf Schwarzkogler
Frank Thiel
Gavin Turk
Martin Walde
Mark Wallinger
Erwin Wurm
Thomas Zipp

ADDRESS

Seilerstätte 16
A-1010 Vienna
AUSTRIA
T: +43.1.513.30.06
F: +43.1.513.30.06.33
www.galerie-krinzinger.at
galeriekrinzinger@chello.at

STAFF

Dr. Ursula Krinzinger
Thomas Krinzinger
Silvia Baltschun
Stanislav Piwowarczyk

Erwin Wurm, **UFO**, 2006, mixed media sculpture, 31 1/5 x 110 1/5 x 216 1/2 inches; 80 x 280 x 550 cm

Kukje Gallery

ARTISTS

Ghada Amer
Jean-Michel Basquiat
Louise Bourgeois
Candice Breitz
Alexander Calder
Duck-Hyun Cho
Kwang-Young Chun
Eva Hesse
Candida Hofer
Kyung Jeon
Yeondoo Jung
Anish Kapoor
Bohnchang Koo
Kwangho Lee
Joan Mitchell
Sungsic Moon

Tim Noble & Sue Webster
YP
Kibong Rhee
Ah-Bin Shim
Kiki Smith

ADDRESS

59-1 Sokyuk-dong
Chongro-ku
110-200 Seoul
KOREA
T: +82.2.735.8449
F: +82.2.735.4580
kukje@kukjegallery.com
www.kukjegallery.com

STAFF

Hyun-Sook Lee, President
Tina Kim
Suzie Kim
Alissa Friedman

Yeondoo Jung, **Location #17**, 2006, c-print, Edition of 5, 48 x 61 1/2 inches; 122 x 156 cm

Kwang-Young Chun, **Aggregation 06-JL033**, 2006, mixed media with Korean Mulberry Paper, 89 x 72 inches; 228 x 183 cm

Yvon Lambert

NEW YORK/PARIS

ARTISTS

Francis Alÿs
Alice Anderson
Carlos Amorales
Carl Andre
Miquel Barceló
Robert Barry
Stanley Brouwn
Mircea Cantor
David Claerbout
Walter Dahn
Berlinde de Bruyckere
Jason Dodge
Spencer Finch
Anna Gaskell
Kendell Geers
Nan Goldin
Douglas Gordon
Jeppe Hein
Jenny Holzer
Jonathan Horowitz
Richard Jackson
Joan Jonas
Isaac Julien
On Kawara
Idris Khan
Anselm Kiefer
Koo Jeong-A
Barbara Kruger

Matthieu Laurette
Bertrand Lavier
Louise Lawler
Zoe Leonard
Claude Lévêque
Sol LeWitt
Glenn Ligon
Miltos Manetas
Christian Marclay
Jonathan Monk
Damian Moppett
Melik Ohanian
Giulio Paolini
Pedro Reyes
Kay Rosen
Charles Sandison
Andres Serrano
David Shrigley
Niele Toroni
Richard Tuttle
Salla Tykkä
Francesco Vezzoli
Ian Wallace
Lawrence Weiner
Ian Wilson
Johannes Wohnseifer
Sislej Xhafa

ADDRESS

550 West 21st Street
New York, NY 10001
USA
T: +1.212.242.3611
F: +1.212.242.3920
newyork@yvon-lambert.com
www.yvon-lambert.com

108, Rue Vieille du Temple
F-75003 Paris
FRANCE
T: +33.1.42.71.09.33
F: +33.1.42.71.87.47
paris@yvon-lambert.com

STAFF

Yvon Lambert, President
Olivier Belot,
    Director General
Rachel D. Vancelette,
    Senior Director
Cornell DeWitt, Director

Charles Sandison, **Reading Glass**, 2005, Computer-generated data projection

Galerie Gebr. Lehmann

DRESDEN

ARTISTS

Tatjana Doll
Markus Draper
Slawomir Elsner
Ellen Harvey
Eberhard Havekost
Hirschvogel
Herbert Hoffmann
Olaf Holzapfel
Martin Honert
Thoralf Knobloch
Dan McCarthy
Martin Mannig
Domingo Molina Cortés
Walther Niedermayr
Frank Nitsche
Suse Weber

ADDRESS

Görlitzer Str. 16
D-01099 Dresden
GERMANY
T: +49.351.801.17.83
F: +49.351.801.49.08
info@galerie-gebr-lehmann.de
www.galerie-gebr-lehmann.de

STAFF

Ralf Lehmann
Frank Lehmann
Karola Matschke
Daniel von Wichelhaus
Grit Dora von Zeschau

Martin Mannig, **Rübenhacker**, 2006, oil and acrylic on canvas, 23 3/5 x 19 7/10 inches; 60 x 50 cm

Lehmann Maupin

NEW YORK

ARTISTS

Stefano Arienti
Kutlug Ataman
Pedro Barbeito
Ashley Bickerton
Ross Bleckner
Christian Curiel
Tracey Emin
Teresita Fernández
Anya Gallaccio
Gilbert & George
Christian Hellmich
Shirazeh Houshiary
Julian LaVerdiere
Mr.
Jun Nguyen-Hatsushiba
Tony Oursler Painting &
    Paper

Maria Pergay
Sergio Prego
Jennifer Steinkamp
Do-Ho Suh
Juergen Teller
Jeffrey Vallance
Adriana Varejão
Suling Wang

ADDRESS

540 West 26th Street
New York, NY 10001
USA
T: +1.212.255.2923
F: +1.212.255.2924
info@lehmannmaupin.com
www.lehmannmaupin.com

STAFF

Rachel Lehmann
David Maupin
Courtney Plummer
Jan Endlich

Mr., **Making Things Right**, 2006, acrylic on canvas, 118 x 177 inches; 300 x 450 cm, (c) 2006 Mr. / Kaikai Kiki Co., Ltd. All Rights Reserved.

ARTISTS

Allora & Calzadilla
Art & Language
Pierre Bismuth
Christine Borland
James Casebere
Tony Cragg
Angela De La Cruz
Richard Deacon
Spencer Finch
Ceal Floyer
Dan Graham
Rodney Graham
Shirazeh Houshiary
Christian Jankowski
Peter Joseph
Anish Kapoor
Igor & Svetlana
  Kopystiansky
John Latham

Tim Lee
Sol Lewitt
Robert Mangold
Jason Martin
Tatsuo Miyajima
Jonathon Monk
John Murphy
Max Neuhaus
Julian Opie
Fernando Ortega
Tony Oursler
Daniele Puppi
Juliao Sarmento
Santiago Sierrra
Jemma Stehli
Lee Ufan
Lawrence Weiner
Richard Wentworth
Jane & Louise Wilson

ADDRESS

29 & 52-54 Bell Street
NW1 5DA London
UNITED KINGDOM
T: +44.20.7724.2739
F: +44.20.7724.7124
contact@lisson.co.uk
www.lisson.co.uk

STAFF

Nicholas Logsdail
Michelle D'Souza
Elly Ketsea
Neil Robert Wenman

Shirazeh Houshiary, **Door**, 2006, Aquacryl and pencil on canvas, 74 3/4 x 74 3/4 inches; 190 x 190 cm, Courtesy of the artist and Lisson Gallery London

Galerie Loevenbruck

PARIS

ARTISTS

Virginie Barré
Alain Declercq
Robert Devriendt
Olivier Blanckart
Daniel Dewar & Gregory
   Gicquel
Blaise Drummond
Vincent Labaume
Arnaud Labelle-Rojoux
Edouard Levé
Philippe Mayaux
Gabor Ösz
Bruno Peinado
Werner Reiterer
Børre Sæthre
Stéphane Sautour

ADDRESS

40, rue de Seine
2 rue de l Echaude
F-75006 Paris
FRANCE
T: +33.1.53.10.85.68
F: +33.1.53.10.89.72
contact@loevenbruck.com
www.loevenbruck.com

STAFF

Alexandra Schillinger
Benoit Moreau
Adrien Lacroix
Elisabeth Fiore, US contact

Philippe Mayaux, **SAVOUREUX DE TOI**, 2006, painted acrylic resin, porcelain and inox, 14 x 16 x 14 inches; 35 x 40 x 35 cm

Mai 36 Galerie   ZURICH

ARTISTS

Franz Ackermann
John Baldessari
Stephan Balkenhol
Matthew Benedict
Troy Brauntuch
Pedro Cabrita Reis
Anke Doberauer
Jürgen Drescher
Roe Ethridge
Pia Fries
Jitka Hanzlová
General Idea
Robert Mapplethorpe
Rita McBride
Harald F. Müller
Matt Mullican
Manfred Pernice
Magnus Plessen

Glen Rubsamen
Christoph Rütimann
Thomas Ruff
Paul Thek
Stefan Thiel
Lawrence Weiner
Rémy Zaugg

ADDRESS

Rämistrasse 37
CH-8001 Zurich
SWITZERLAND
T: +41.44.261.68.80
F: +41.44.261.68.81
mail@mai36.com
www.mai36.com

STAFF

Victor Gisler
Luigi Kurmann
Gabriela Walther

Matt Mullican, **Untitled (Direct Casts: Cosmology)**, 2006, 2 parts, cast metal, steel vitrine with glass, 16 3/4 x 16 3/4 x 6 1/8 inches each; 42.5 x 42.5 x 15.5 cm (with certificate)

Matthew Marks Gallery

NEW YORK

ARTISTS

Robert Adams
Darren Almond
David Armstrong
Nayland Blake
Willem de Kooning
Peter Fischli David Weiss
Peter Cain
Lucian Freud
Katharina Fritsch
Robert Gober
Nan Goldin
Andreas Gursky
Jonathan Hammer

Martin Honert
Peter Hujar
Gary Hume
Jasper Johns
Ellsworth Kelly
Inez van Lamsweerde
Brice Marden
Roy McMakin
Ken Price
Charles Ray
Ugo Rondinone
Tony Smith
Terry Winters

ADDRESS

523 West 24th Street
New York, NY 10011
USA

Also:
522 West 22nd Street
521 West 21st Street

T: +1.212.243.0200
F: +1.212.243.0047
info@matthewmarks.com
www.matthewmarks.com

STAFF

Sabrina Buell
Cristopher Canizares
Stephanie Dorsey
Jeffrey Peabody

Ken Price, **Slope**, 2006, fired and painted clay, 12 1/2 x 18 1/2 x 13 1/2 inches; 32 x 47 x 34 cm

Sara Meltzer Gallery   NEW YORK

ARTISTS

Jan Albers
Roger Andersson
Felipe Barbosa
Lee Boroson
Andrea Bowers
Margarita Cabrera
Jeremy Dickinson
Moyna Flannigan
Peter Friedl
Neil Goldberg
Nina Katchadourian
Enrique Martinez Celaya
Jason Middlebrook
Edgar Orlaineta

Shannon Plumb
Daniela Steinfeld
Jude Tallichet
Type A

ADDRESS

525-531 West 26th Street
New York, NY 10001
USA
T: +1.212.727.9330
F: +1.212.630.0397
info@sarameltzergallery.com
www.sarameltzergallery.com

STAFF

Sara Meltzer
Jeffrey Walkowiak
Rachel Gugelberger
Adria Marquez

Moyna Flannigan, **works from the series 'A Pie in the Kisser'**, 2005, Conte pastel on Somerset paper; dimensions variable

Galerie Kamel Mennour

PARIS

ARTISTS

Adel Abdessemed
Nobuyoshi Araki
David Armstrong
Roger Ballen
Marie Bovo
Daniel Buren
Fabien
Leo Fabrizio
Alberto Garcia-Alix
Jason Glasser
Janine Gordon
Peter Granser
Guido Mocafico
Daido Moriyama
Martin Parr
Christine Rebet

Robin Rhode
Zineb Sedira
Miri Segal
Stephen Shore
Djamel Tatah

ADDRESS

60, rue Mazarine
F-75006 Paris
FRANCE
T: +33.1.56.24.03.63
F: +33.1.56.24.03.64
contact@galerie
     mennour.com
www.galeriemennour.com

STAFF

Kamel Mennour
Marie-Sophie Eiché

Adel Abdessemed, **Séparation**, 2006, C-print, 40 2/3 x 35 3/8 inches; 103 x 90 cm

ARTISTS

Olaf Breuning
Andreas Hofer
Isaac Julien
Mike Kelley
Martin Kippenberger
Louise Lawler
Robert Longo
Yuri Masnyj
Keegan McHargue
Lucy McKenzie
John Miller
Paulina Olowska
Tony Oursler
Sterling Ruby
Jim Shaw

Cindy Sherman
Gary Simmons
Andreas Slominski
Catherine Sullivan
TJ Wilcox

ADDRESS

519 West 24th Street
New York, NY 10011
USA
T: +1.212.206.7100
F: +1.212.337.0070
gallery@metropictures
  gallery.com
www.metropictures
  gallery.com

STAFF

Janelle Reiring
Helene Winer
Tom Heman
Allison Card
Manuela Mozo

Louise Lawler, **I've Always Liked That Picture**, 2005/2006, cibachrome mounted on aluminum box, 23 1/4 x 23 1/4 inches; 59.1 x 59.1 cm, Edition of 5

Galerie Meyer Kainer

ARTISTS

Vanessa Beecroft
John Bock
Agata Bogacka
Olaf Breuning
Plamen Dejanoff
gelatin
Liam Gillick
Dan Graham
Mary Heilmann
Christian Jankowski
Michael Krebber
Marcin Maciejowski
Sarah Morris
Yoshitomo Nara
Walter Niedermayr
Walter Obholzer

Jorge Pardo
Raymond Pettibon
Mathias Poledna
Martina Steckholzer
Beat Streuli
Wolfgang Tillmans
Franz West
T. J. Wilcox
Heimo Zobernig

ADDRESS

Eschenbachgasse 9
A-1050 Vienna
AUSTRIA
T: +43.15.85.7277
F: +43.15.85.7539
info@meyerkainer.com
www.meyerkainer.com

STAFF

Renate Kainer
Christian Meyer
Michele Ziesel

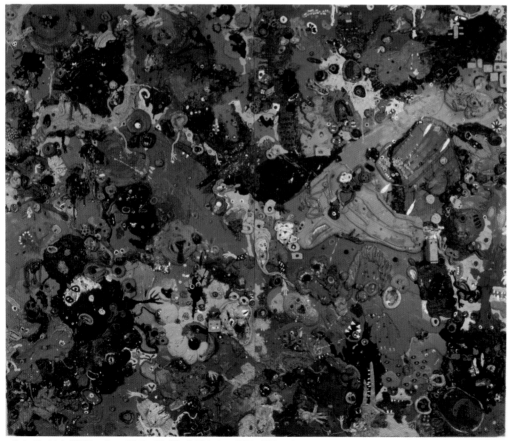

gelatin, **Untitled**, 2006, collage, 81.5 x 98.43 x 5.12 inches; 207 x 250 x 13 cm

Meyer Riegger Galerie   KARLSRUHE

ARTISTS

Franz Ackermann
Armin Boehm
Jeanne Faust
Sebastian Hammwöhner
Isabell Heimerdinger
Uwe Henneken
Anna Lea Hucht
Dani Jakob
Korpys/Löffler
Kalin Lindena
Jan Mancuska
Meuser
John Miller
Helen Mirra
Jonathan Monk
Daniel Roth

Glen Rubsamen
Silke Schatz
David Thorpe
Gabriel Vormstein
Corinne Wasmuht
Eric Wesley

ADDRESS

Klauprechtstrasse 22
D-76137 Karlsruhe
GERMANY
T: +49.721.821292
F: +49.721.9822141
info@meyer-riegger.de
www.meyer-riegger.de

STAFF

Jochen Meyer, Owner
Thomas Riegger, Owner
Julia Hölz, Director

Jan Mancuska, **The Painting Vol. III**, 2006, enamel on canvas, plexi glass, 39 3/8 x 39 3/8 inches; 100 x 100 cm

Robert Miller Gallery

ARTISTS

Ai Weiwei
Diane Arbus
Robert Greene
Bill Henson
Michael Kalmbach
Ola Kolehmainen
Lee Krasner
Sven Kroner
Yayoi Kusama
John Lurie
Alice Neel
Walter Niedermayr
Patricia Piccinini
Milton Resnick
Patti Smith

Pierre Soulages
Mayumi Terada
Bernar Venet
Tom Wesselmann

ADDRESS

524 West 26th Street
New York, NY 10001
USA
T: +1.212.336.4774
F: +1.212.366.4454
rmg@robertmillergallery.com
www.robertmillergallery.com

STAFF

Betsy Wittenborn Miller,
    Director

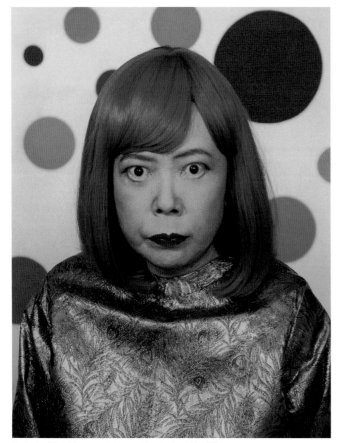

Portrait of Yayoi Kusama, Courtesy the studio of Yayoi Kusama

Yayoi Kusama, **Shooting Star**, 2006, mirrors and incadescent bulbs, 84 x 191 x 84 inches; 213.3 x 485 x 213.3 cm

Milliken

ARTISTS

Bigert and Bergström
Brian Conley
Per Enoksson
Felix Gmelin
Bill Jacobson
Lisa Jeannin
Kristina Jansson
Matti Kallioinen
Robert Lucander
Anna Ling
Lars Nilsson
Åsa Nylén
Mattias Nordéus
Lars Siltberg

Mari Slaattelid
Fredrik Söderberg
Hanna Tingsgård
Olav Westphalen

ADDRESS

Luntmakargatan 78
S-11351 Stockholm
SWEDEN
T: +46.8.673.7010
F: +46.8.673.7020
M: + 46.70.966.6565
mail@millikengallery.com
www.millikengallery.com

STAFF

Lina Åkerlund
Aldy Milliken
Liv Stoltz

Kristina Jansson, **Burnt Museum**, 2006, oil on canvas, 70 x 86 2/3 inches; 180 x 220 cm, Photo credit: Jean-Baptiste Béranger

Felix Gmelin, **Flatbed Blue Curtain**, Installation view Portikus Gallery, Frankfurt am Main, Video Projection, 2004, 236 minutes, Photo Credit: Wolfgang Günzel

Victoria Miro Gallery   LONDON

ARTISTS

Doug Aitken
Hernan Bas
Varda Caivano
Anne Chu
Verne Dawson
Thomas Demand
Peter Doig
William Eggleston
Inka Essenhigh
Ian Hamilton Finlay
David Harrison
Alex Hartley
Chantal Joffe
Isaac Julien
Idris Khan
John Kørner

Udomsak Krisanamis
Dawn Mellor
Tracey Moffatt
Hiroko Nakao
Alice Neel
Chris Ofili
Jacco Olivier
Grayson Perry
Tal R
Raqib Shaw
Conrad Shawcross
Adriana Varejão
Suling Wang
Stephen Willats
Francesca Woodman

ADDRESS

16 Wharf Road
N1 7RW London
UNITED KINGDOM
T: +44.20.7336.8109
F: +44.20.7251.5596
info@victoria-miro.com
www.victoria-miro.com

STAFF

Victoria Miro
Glenn Scott Wright
Andrew Silewicz
James Lindon

Peter Doig, **Masqueraders**, 2006, giclée and silk screen on Somerset Velvet Enhanced 255 gsm paper 25 1/8 x 20 3/8 inches; 63.7 cm x 51.9 cm, edition of 250 plus 20 artist's proofs

ARTISTS

Tjorg Douglas Beer
Anthony Caro
Natalie Frank
Jack Goldstein
Leon Kossoff
Justine Kurland
Alexander Liberman
Roy Lichtenstein
Christopher Miner
Enoc Perez
Martha Rosler
Jessica Stockholder
Jack Tworkov
Paul Winstanley

ADDRESS

534 West 26th Street
New York, NY 10001
USA
T: +1.212.744.7400
F: +1.212.744.7401
info@miandn.com
www.miandn.com

1018 Madison Avenue
New York, NY 10021
USA

STAFF

David Nash
Lucy Mitchell-Innes
Jay Gorney

Natalie Frank, **Portrait with Owl and Birds**, 2006, oil on canvas, 74 3/4 x 44 1/4 inches; 189.9 x 112.4 cm

The Modern Institute

GLASGOW

ARTISTS

Dirk Bell
Martin Boyce
Jeremy Deller
Urs Fischer
Kim Fisher
Luke Fowler
Henrik Håkansson
Mark Handforth
Richard Hughes
Chris Johanson
Andrew Kerr
Jim Lambie
Victoria Morton
Scott Myles
Toby Paterson
Simon Periton
Mary Redmond

Anselm Reyle
Eva Rothschild
Monika Sosnowska
Simon Starling
Katja Strunz
Tony Swain
Spencer Sweeney
Joanne Tatham and Tom
   O'Sullivan
Pádraig Timoney
Hayley Tompkins
Sue Tompkins
Cathy Wilkes
Michael Wilkinson
Richard Wright

ADDRESS

Suite 6
73 Robertson Street
G2 8QD Glasgow
SCOTLAND, UK
T: +44.141.2483711
F: +44.141.2483280
mail@themodern
   institute.com
www.themodern
   institute.com

STAFF

Toby Webster
Andrew Hamilton

Martin Boyce, **Electric Trees and Telephone Booth Conversations**, (Installation view) 2006, Frac Des Pays De La Loire

Murray Guy

NEW YORK

ARTISTS

Matthew Buckingham
Francis Cape
Alejandro Cesarco
Kota Ezawa
Noriko Furunishi
Munro Galloway
Matthew Higgs
An-My Lê
Ann Lislegaard
Barbara Probst
Beat Streuli
Shirley Tse

ADDRESS

453 West 17th Street
New York, NY 10011
USA
T: +1.212.463.7372
F: +1.212.463.7319
info@murrayguy.com
www.murrayguy.com

STAFF

Janice Guy
Margaret Murray

Barbara Probst, **Exposure #39: N.Y.C. 545 8th Avenue, 03.23.06, 1:17p.m.**, 2006, Ultrachrome ink on cotton paper, 2 parts: 66 x 44 inches; 168 x 112 cm

Galerie Christian Nagel

COLOGNE/BERLIN

ARTISTS

Kai Althoff
Kader Attia
Nairy Baghramian
Lutz Braun
Merlin Carpenter
Clegg & Guttman
Andreas Diefenbach
Mark Dion
Diego Fernandez
Andrea Fraser
Renée Green
Rachel Harrison
Kalin Lindena
Hans-Jörg Mayer
Christian-Philipp Müller
Stefan Müller
Nils Norman
Josephine Pryde
Sterling Ruby

Cornelius Quabeck
Catherine Sullivan
Jan Timme
Stephen Willats
Joseph Zehrer
Gang Zhao
Heimo Zobernig

ADDRESS

Richard-Wagner-Strasse 28
D-50674 Cologne
GERMANY
T: +49.221.257.0591
F: +49.221.257.0592
cn.koeln@galerie-nagel.de
www.galerie-nagel.de

Weydinger Strasse 2/4
D-10178 Berlin
GERMANY
T: +49.30.400.42.641
F: +49.30.400.42.642
cn.berlin@galerie-nagel.de

STAFF

Christian Nagel, Owner
Isabelle Erben, Berlin
Susanne Prinz, Berlin
Florian Baron, Cologne
Bettina Rheinbay, Cologne

Michael Krebber, **Installation view Galerie Christian Nagel**, Art Chicago 1993

Nature Morte

ARTISTS

Anju Dodiya
Atul Dodiya
Anita Dube
Sheela Gowda
Shilpa Gupta
Subodh Gupta
Ranbir Kaleka
Jitish Kallat
Bharti Kher
Bari Kumar
Nalini Malani
Pushpamala N.
Manisha Parekh
Jagannath Panda
Justin Ponmany

Rashid Rana
Raqs Media Collective
Ravinder Reddy
Mithu Sen
Dayanita Singh
Nataraj Sharma
Thukral & Tagra
Hema Upadhyay

ADDRESS

A-1 Neeti Bagh
110049 New Delhi
INDIA
T: +91.11.4174.0215
F: +91.11.4176.4608
info@naturemorte.com
www.naturemorte.com

STAFF

Peter Nagy
Arani Bose
Shumita Bose
Steven V. Pacia

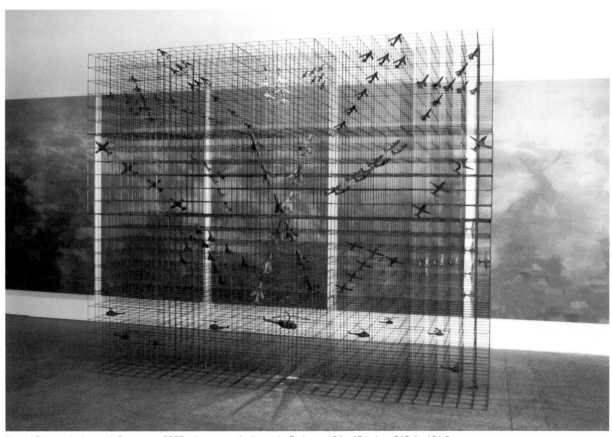

Nataraj Sharma, background: **Departure**, 2005, oil on canvas in six panels, Each panel 84 x 48 inches; 213.4 x 121.9 cm
foreground: **Air Show**, 2005, cast and welded iron sculpture, 120 x 96 x 24 inches; 304.8 x 243.8 x 60.9 cm

Carolina Nitsch

NEW YORK

ARTISTS	ADDRESS	STAFF

Louise Bourgeois
Vija Celmins
E.V. Day
Richard Dupont
Olafur Eliasson
Douglas Gordon
Donald Judd
Bruce Nauman
Olaf Nicolai
Richard Prince
Dieter Roth
Ed Ruscha
Alyson Shotz
Laurie Simmons
Hiroshi Sugimoto
Jeff Wall

101 Wooster Street
New York, NY 10012
USA
(mail)

537 Greenwich Street
New York, NY 10013
USA
(gallery)

T: +1.212.463.0610
F: +1.212.463.0614
acnitsch@aol.com
www.artnet.com/
    cnitsch.html

Carolina Nitsch
Dieter von Graffenried
Brian Rumbolo

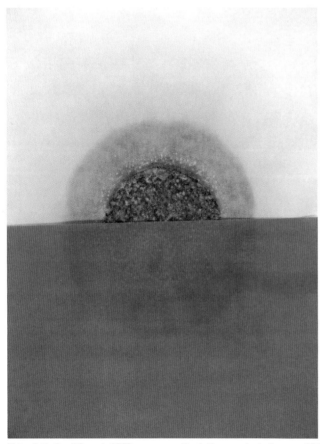

Dieter Roth, **Small Sunset**, 1968, sausage on blue/white paper in plastic cover. 17 1/2 x 13 inches; 43 x 32 cm

Galleria Franco Noero

TURIN

ARTISTS

Tom Burr
Jeff Burton
Neil Campbell
Adam Chodzko
Lara Favaretto
Henrik Håkansson
Arturo Herrera
Gabriel Kuri
Jim Lambie
Muntean/Rosenblum
Mike Nelson
Henrik Olesen
Steven Shearer
Simon Starling
Costa Veoe
Francesco Vezzoli
Eric Wesley

ADDRESS

Via Giolitti 52A
I-10123 Turin
ITALY
T: +39.011.882.208
F: +39.011.1970.3024
info@franconoero.com
www.franconoero.com

STAFF

Franco Noero
Pierpaolo Falone
Luisa Salvi Del Pero
Antoine Levi

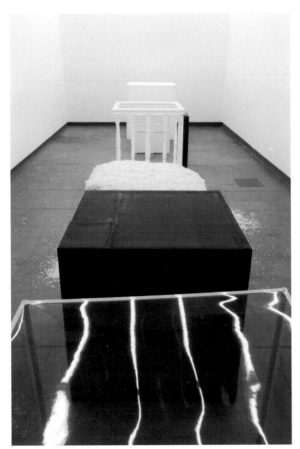

'Al Cubo', **installation view at Galleria Franco Noero**, June-July 2006, Works by Tom Burr, Lara Favaretto, Gabriel Kuri, Jim Lambie, Henrik Olesen, Eric Wesley

David Nolan Gallery

ARTISTS	ADDRESS	STAFF
Richard Artschwager	560 Broadway #604	David Nolan
William N. Copley	New York, NY 10012	Katherine Chan
Steve DiBenedetto	USA	
Carroll Dunham	T: +1.212.925.6190	
Ian Hamilton Finlay	F: +1.212.334.9139	
Victoria Gitman	info@davidnolangallery.com	
Mel Kendrick	www.davidnolangallery.com	
Barry Le Va		
Alice Maher		
Jim Nutt		
Albert Oehlen		
Erwin Pfrang		
Alexander Ross		
Peter Saul		
Miroslav Tichý		
Joe Zucker		

Miroslav Tichý, **Untitled**, ca. 1950's-1980's, unique vintage photograph with artist's frame, 8 1/2 x 11 1/2 inches; 21.6 x 29.2 cm

Ian Hamilton Finlay, **Aphrodite de la Terreur (Aphrodite of the Terror)**, 1987, plaster and ribbon, 63 x 18 x 21 inches; 160 x 45.7 x 53.3 cm

PaceWildenstein

ADDRESS

32 East 57th Street
New York, NY 10022
USA
T: +1.212.421.3292
F: +1.212.421.835
info@pacewildenstein.com
www.pacewildenstein.com

534 West 25th Street
New York, NY 10001
USA
T: +1.212.929.7000
F: +1.212.929.7001

545 West 22nd Street
New York NY 10011
USA
T: +1.212.989.4258
F: +1.212.989.4263

Kiki Smith, **Fox on the Ground**, 2004, bronze, 41 1/2 x 96 1/4 x 2 inches; 105.4 x 244.5 x 5.1 cm, Edition of 3 + 1 AP

Joel Shapiro, **Untitled**, 2001 (2005), bronze, Artist's Proof 9 1/2 x 3 1/2 x 2 inches; 24.1 x 8.3 x 5.1 cm

Patrick Painter, Inc.

ARTISTS

Bas Jan Ader
Hope Atherton
Georg Baselitz
Glenn Brown
André Butzer
Valie Export
Bernard Frize
Francesca Gabbiani
Jörg Immendorff
Larry Johnson
Mike Kelley
Won Ju Lim
Sebastian Ludwig
Ivan Morley
Albert Oehlen
Kenny Scharf
Christian Schumann

Jim Shaw
Marnie Weber
Li Wei
Peter Wu
Thomas Zipp
Sigmar Polke,
Ed Ruscha,
Andy Warhol works available

ADDRESS

West Gallery
2525 Michigan Avenue
Unit B2
Santa Monica, CA 90404
USA
T: +1.310.264.5988
F: +1.310.264.5998
info@patrickpainter.com
www.patrickpainter.com

East Gallery
2525 Michigan Avenue
Unit A8
Santa Monica, CA 90404
USA
T: +1.310.828.3793
F: +1.310.453.6354

STAFF

Patrick Painter,
  Owner/Director
Daniel Congdon, Director
Edward Chu, Sales Director

Mike Kelley, **Garbage Bag #2**, 1989, acrylic on paper, 41 1/4 x 34 inches; 101.6 x 81.3 cm

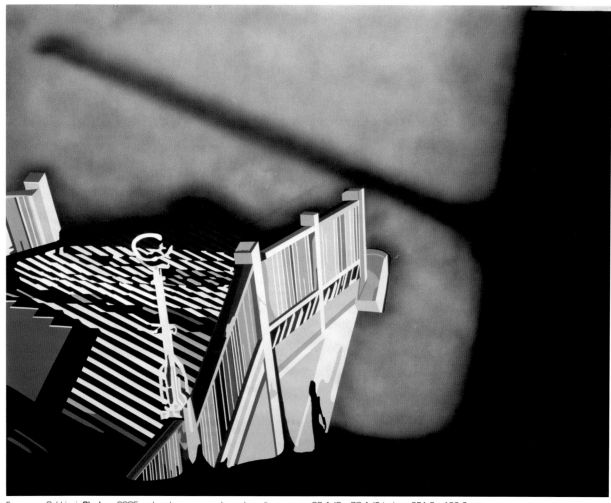

Francesca Gabbiani, **Slasher**, 2005, colored paper, gouache and acrylic on paper, 99 1/8 x 77 1/2 inches; 251.8 x 196.9 cm

Jim Shaw, **Dream Object (Vise Head)**, bronze, wood, steel, 47 x 54 x 35 1/2 inches; 119.4 x 137.2 x 90.2 cm

Paul Morrison, **EPITHILIUM**, 2006, screenprint, edition of 45, 51 3/4 x 39 3/4 inches; 131.5 x 99.5 cm

Peres Projects

LOS ANGELES/BERLIN

ARTISTS

assume vivid astro focus
Dan Attoe
Chris Ballantyne
Dan Colen
Liz Craft
Folkert De Jong
Amie Dicke
Kaye Donachie
Matt Greene
John Kleckner
Terence Koh
Bruce LaBruce
Kirstine Roepstorff
Dean Sameshima
Mark Titchner

ADDRESS

969 Chung King Road
Los Angeles, CA 90012
USA
T: +1.213.617.1100
F: +1.213.617.1141
info@peresprojects.com
www.peresprojects.com

Schlesische Strasse 26
D-10997 Berlin
GERMANY
T: +49.30.6162.6962
F: +49.30.6162.7066
berlin@peresprojects.com

STAFF

Javier Peres
Mary Blair Taylor
Sarah Walzer
Richard Lidinsky
Margherita Belaief
Eric Huebsch
Wilson Chang
Ethan Hayes-Chute

left: John Kleckner, **Untitled**, 2006, drawing, ink on paper, 4 x 3 1/2 inches; 10.2 x 8.9 cm
right: Terence Koh, **installation view of installation at Kunsthalle Zurich**, 2006

Galerie Emmanuel Perrotin

ARTISTS

Chiho Aoshima
Daniel Arsham
Bhakti Baxter
Sophie Calle
Maurizio Cattelan
Wim Delvoye
Eric Duyckaerts
Elmgreen & Dragset
Lionel Esteve
Léandro Erlich
Naomi Fisher
Bernard Frize
Giuseppe Gabellone
Gelitin
Kolkoz
Guy Limone

Jin Meyerson
Mr.
Takashi Murakami
Martin Oppel
Jean-Michel Othoniel
Paola Pivi
Terry Richardson
Cristina Lei Rodriguez
Aya Takano
Piotr Uklanski
Xavier Veilhan
Peter Zimmermann

ADDRESS

76, rue de Turenne
F-75003 Paris
FRANCE
T: +33.1.42.16.79.79
F: +33.1.42.16.79.74
info-paris@galerie
    perrotin.com
www.galerieperrotin.com

194 North West
30th Street
Miami, FL 33127
USA
T: +1.305.573.2130
F: +1.305.573.0595
info-miami@galerie
    perrotin.com

STAFF

Emmanuel Perrotin,
    Director
Peggy Leboeuf, Director
Gen Watanabe, Director
Nathalie Brambilla,
    Assistant
Etsuko Nakajima, Assistant

Kolkoz, **Film de vacances, Formentera**, 2006, wood, paint, dvd, video player, 71 x 81 x 78 inches; 180.3 x 205.7 x 198.1 cm

Friedrich Petzel Gallery   NEW YORK

ARTISTS

Cosima von Bonin
Matthew Brannon
Troy Brauntuch
Keith Edmier
Andrea Fraser
Wade Guyton
Georg Herold
Charline von Heyl
Allan McCollum
Sarah Morris
Jorge Pardo
Philippe Parreno
Stephen Prina
Jon Pylypchuk
Dirk Skreber
Nicola Tyson

ADDRESS

535-537 West 22nd Street
New York, NY 10011
USA
T: +1.212.680.9467
F: +1.212.680.9473
info@petzel.com
www.petzel.com

STAFF

Friedrich Petzel
Maureen Sarro
Andrea Teschke

Sarah Morris, **Robert Towne**, 2006, Lever House, New York, gloss paint on ceiling, Photo: Seong Kwon, courtesy Public Art Fund

ARTISTS

Dawn Clements
Brian Dewan
James Esber
Jane Fine
Tony Fitzpatrick
Kate Gilmore
Jonathan Herder
Kim Jones
Mark Lombardi
Ati Maier
John J. O'Connor
Jonathan Schipper
Ward Shelley
Tavares Strachan
Jim Torok
Daniel Zeller

ADDRESS

177 North 9th Street
Brooklyn, NY 11211
USA
T: +1.718.599.2144
F: +1.718.599.1666
info@pierogi2000.com
www.pierogi2000.com

Spinnereistrasse 7
Halle 10
D-04179 Leipzig
GERMANY
T: +49.341.241.90.80
F: +49.341.241.90.82
info@pierogileipzig.com

STAFF

Joe Amrhein,
    Co-Owner/Director
Susan Swenson,
    Co-Owner
Summer Guthery,
    Gallery Manager, Brooklyn
Joshua Weintraub,
    Gallery Assistant,
    Brooklyn
Justin Amrhein,
    Gallery Assistant,
    Brooklyn
Jason Starkie,
    Gallery Director, Leipzig
Christina Linden,
    Assistant Director, Leipzig

Kate Gilmore, **Anything...**, 2006, 12 minutes, 24 seconds, DVD, Edition of 5

Plan B

CLUJ

ARTISTS

Alexandra Croitoru
Adrian Ghenie
Victor Man
Szilard Miklos
Ciprian Muresan
Barbara Musil
Miklós Onucsán
Cristi Pogacean
Serban Savu
Gabriela Vanga

ADDRESS

Str. Albert Einstein 14
400045 Cluj
ROMANIA
T: +40.742.504901
contact@plan-b.ro
www.plan-b.ro

STAFF

Mihai Pop
Tereza Anton

Victor Man, **Untitled**, 2006, assemblage, 4 - parts, mixed medium, dimensions variable

Galerie Praz-Delavallade

PARIS

ARTISTS

Edgar Arceneaux
Marc Bauer
Andrea Bowers
Roderick Buchanan
Valentin Carron
Marc Couturier
Philippe Decrauzat
Sam Durant
Jim Isermann
Natacha Lesueur
John Miller
Shahryar Nashat
Adi Nes
Robyn O'Neil
Amy O'Neill
Roman Opalka

Mai-Thu Perret
Daniel Pflumm
John Pilson
Monique Prieto
Dario Robleto
Brett Cody Rogers
Analia Saban
Yvan Salomone
Erik Schmidt
Jim Shaw
Vedovamazzei
Marnie Weber

ADDRESS

28, rue Louise Weiss
F-75013 Paris
FRANCE
T: +33.1.45.86.20.00
F: +33.1.45.86.20.10
gallery@praz-delavallade.com
www.praz-delavallade.com

STAFF

Bruno Delavallade, Owner
René-Julien Praz, Owner
Eléonore Lambertie,
   Director

Robyn O'Neil, **Ordinary men have hearts that hunt these sacred sprouts no matter the hour, for they need this calm**, graphite on paper, 80 x 80 inches; 203 x 203 cm

Valentin Carron, **Forza Ethiopia**, 2006, carved polyurethane, epoxy, metal, paint, 86 5/8 x 28 3/8 x 28 3/8 inches; 220 x 72 x 72 cm

Produzentengalerie Hamburg

HAMBURG

ARTISTS

Tjorg Douglas Beer
Ulla von Brandenburg
Jonas Burgert
Beate Gütschow
Bethan Huws
Gustav Kluge
Thomas Scheibitz
Thomas Schütte
Norbert Schwontkowski
Andreas Slominski
Nicole Wermers

ADDRESS

Admiralitätstraße 71
D-20459 Hamburg
GERMANY
T: +49.40.37.82.32
F: +49.40.36.33.04
info@produzenten
    galerie.com
www.produzenten
    galerie.com

STAFF

Jürgen Vorrath, Director
Rainer Noeres, Director
Harald Rüggeberg,
    Director
Peter Sander, Director
Anna-Catharina Gebbers,
    Assistant
Tanja Maka, Assistant
Kerstin Stakemeier,
    Assistant

Thomas Schütte, **Haus für den schüchternen Verleger**, Architektur-Modelle, 2006, Installation View

The Project

NEW YORK

ARTISTS

José Damasceno
Coco Fusco
Maria Elena González
Barkley Hendricks
Nic Hess
Glenn Kaino
Kimsooja
Daniel Joseph Martinez
Julie Mehretu
Aernout Mik
Kori Newkirk
Yoshua Okon
Geof Oppenheimer
Paul Pfeiffer
William Pope L.
Jessica Rankin
Peter Rostovsky

Tracey Rose
Cristián Silva
Steven Vitiello
Chen Xiaoyun

ADDRESS

37 West 57th Street
Third Floor
New York, NY 10019
USA
T: +1.212.688.1585
F: +1.212.688.1589
mail@elproyecto.com
www.elproyecto.com

STAFF

Christian Haye
Renaud Proch
Giovanni Garcia-Fenech
Lizzy Cross

William Pope.L, **Four Horsemen of the Apocalypse (25)**, 2006, Fugiflex digital C Print, Edition 6 + 2AP, 48 x 72 inches; 121.92 x 182.88 cm

Galerie Almine Rech

PARIS/BRUSSELS

ARTISTS

Rita Ackermann
Nobuyoshi Araki
Matias Becker
Tom Burr
Damien Cadio
Serge Comte
Philip-Lorca diCorcia
Anita Dube
John Giorno
Wenda Gu
Mark Handforth
Peter Joseph
Johannes Kahrs
Joseph Kosuth
Ange Leccia
John McCracken
Kenneth Noland
Sven Pahlsson

Tobias Putrih
Matt Saunders
Nathaniel Rackowe
Anselm Reyle
Zbigniew Rogalski
Ugo Rondinone
Bruno Rousseaud
Hedi Slimane
Annelies Strba
Vincent Szarek
John Tremblay
Tatiana Trouvé
Gavin Turk
James Turrell
Stephen Vitiello
Miwa Yanagi

ADDRESS

19, rue de Saintonge
F-75003 Paris
FRANCE
T: +33.1.45.83.71.90
F: +33.1.45.70.91.30
a.rech@galeriealmine
    rech.com
www.galeriealminerech.com

11 avenue Victoria
B-1000 Brussels
BELGIUM

STAFF

PARIS
Thomas Dryll, Director
Renaud Pillon, Co-Director
Marie-Laure Gilles,
    Assistant
Soizic Oger, Assistant
Céline Guillemet, Assistant
Benjamin Rivière, Assistant
Antoine Aguilar, Registrar

BRUSSELS
Almine Rech, Owner
Bérénice Chef, Director

Zbigniew Rogalski, **How my friend sees a plane**, 2006, oil on canvas, 39 3/8 x 55 1/8 inches; 100 x 140 cm

Daniel Reich Gallery

ARTISTS

Scoli Acosta
Hernan Bas
Black Leotard Front
Michael Cline
Sean Dack
Amy Gartrell
Delia Gonzalez +
   Gavin R. Russom
Christian Holstad
Anya Kielar
Birgit Megerle
Paul P.
Scott Reeder
Tyson Reeder

ADDRESS

537 A West 23 Street
New York, NY 10011
USA
T: +1.212.924.4949
F: +1.212.924.6224
gallery@danielreichgallery.com
www.danielreichgallery.com

STAFF

John McCord
Guillaume Rouchon

Christian Holstad, **The Terms of Endearment (Installation View)**, 2006, photo credit: Steven Brooke

Michael Cline, **Untitled**, 2006, charcoal on paper, 18 x 24 inches; 45.7 x 61 cm

Rivington Arms

NEW YORK

ARTISTS

Mathew Cerletty
Darren Bader
John Finneran
Lansing-Dreiden
Hanna Liden
Carter Mull
Dash Snow
Pinar Yolacan

ADDRESS

4 East 2nd Street
1st Floor
New York, NY 10003
USA
T: +1.646.654.3213
F: +1.212.475.1801
info@rivingtonarms.com
www.rivingtonarms.com

STAFF

Melissa Bent, Co-Director
Mirabelle Marden,
    Co-Director

Lansing-Dreiden, **Suggested Arrangement - III (detail)**, 2006, 13 1/4 X 28 1/2 inches; 33.7 x 72.4 cm, Book Pages

Galerie Thaddaeus Ropac

PARIS/SALZBURG

ARTISTS

Donald Baechler
Georg Baselitz
Tony Cragg
Elger Esser
Sylvie Fleury
Gilbert & George
Antony Gormley
Alex Katz
Anselm Kiefer
Robert Mapplethorpe
Jason Martin
Jack Pierson
Lisa Ruyter
Tom Sachs
David Salle
Andy Warhol

ADDRESS

7, rue Debelleyme
F-75003 Paris
FRANCE
T: +33.1.42.72.99.00
F: +33.1.42.72 61 66
galerie@ropac.net
www.ropac.net

Mirabellplatz 2
A-5020 Salzburg
AUSTRIA
T: +43.662.881.393
F: +43.662.881.3939
office@ropac.at

STAFF

Thaddaeus Ropac
Jill Silverman van
   Coenegrachts
Arne Ehmann
Bénédicte Burrus
Elena Bortolotti

Jack Pierson, **Installation View**, Paris 2006

ARTISTS

Marina Abramovic
Ivan Bazak
Vanessa Beecroft
Alberto Burri
Enrico Castellani
Clegg & Guttmann
Gino De Dominicis
Tessa M. Den Uyl
Esc-Quarta Pittura
Granular Synthesis
Andreas Gursky
Gary Hill
Douglas Huebler
Alfredo Jaar
Mimmo Jodice
Donald Judd
Ilya Kabakov
William Kentridge

Anselm Kiefer
Joseph Kosuth
Hendik Krawen
Sven Kroner
Tom Mc Grath
Reinhard Mucha
Marzia Migliora
Ottonella Mocellin-Nicola
  Pellegrini
Sabah Naim
Shirin Neshat
Michelangelo Pistoletto
Thomas Ruff
Franco Scognamiglio
Haim Steinbach
Dre' Wapenaar
Christopher Williams
Tobias Zielony

ADDRESS

Via Vannella Gaetani, 12
I-80121 Naples
ITALY
T: +39.81.7643619
F: +39.81.7644213
info@gallerialiarumma.it
www.gallerialiarumma.it

Via Solferino, 44
I-20121 Milan
ITALY
T: +39.02.29000101

STAFF

Lia Rumma
Paola Potena
Lodovica Busiri Vici
Francesca Boenzi

William Kentridge, **Porter series: Asia Minor**, 2006, mohair silk and embroidery, 98 3/8 x 137 3/4 inches; 250 x 350 cm, Courtesy Lia Rumma

ARTISTS

Hernan Bas
Iona Rozeal Brown
John White Cerasulo
Sue de Beer
John Espinosa
Anthony Goicolea
Soo Kim
Henning Kles
Jörg Lozek
Johan Nobell
Chloe Piene
Adam Putnam
David Schnell
Macrae Semans

ADDRESS

2762 South
La Cienega Boulevard
Los Angeles, CA 90034
USA
T: +1.310.280.0111
F: +1.310.280.0808
info@sandronirey.com
www.sandronirey.com

STAFF

Tara Sandroni
Kristin Rey
Nu Nguyen
Lauren Miller

Jörg Lozek, **Der Siebenschlafer**, 2005, oil on canvas, 87 x 110 inches; 220 x 280 cm

Galerie Aurel Scheibler

BERLIN

ARTISTS

Peter Cain
Öyvind Fahlström
Anthony Goicolea
Christian Holstad
Stefan Löffelhardt
Sarah Morris
Ernst Wilhelm Nay
Jack Pierson
Bridget Riley
Peter Saul
Claudia Schink
Rachel Selekman
Peter Stauss
Billy Sullivan
Alessandro Twombly

Christoph Wedding
Erwin Wurm
Joe Zucker

ADDRESS

Witzlebenplatz 4
D-14057 Berlin
GERMANY
T: +49.30.3030.1329
F: +49.30.3011.2420
office@aurelscheibler.com
www.aurelscheibler.com

STAFF

Marie Graftieaux
Alexander Hattwig
Dr. Brigitte Schlüter

Peter Stauss, **The blind leading the blind**, 2006, oil and gouache on cardboard, 78 3/4 x 59 1/2 inches; 200 x 150 cm

Galerie Thomas Schulte

BERLIN

ARTISTS

Richard Deacon
Mark Francis
Alfredo Jaar
Idris Khan
Jonathan Lasker
Robert Mapplethorpe
Fabian Marcaccio
Gordon Matta-Clark
Allan McCollum
Jacco Olivier
Albrecht Schnider
Iris Schomaker
Katharina Sieverding
Jessica Stockholder
Stephanie Snider
Juan Uslé

ADDRESS

Charlottenstraße 24
D-10117 Berlin
GERMANY
T: +49.30.2060.8990
F: +49.30.2060.89910
mail@galeriethomas
   schulte.de
www.galeriethomas
   schulte.de

STAFF

Thomas Schulte
Björn Alfers
Melanie Heit
Elisabeth Ouillon
Alexandra Schott

Allan McCollum, **Shape**, 2006, Corian, 20 1/2 x 13 3/8 x 6 7/10 inches; 52 x 34 x 17 cm, Installation view

Jack Shainman Gallery

NEW YORK

ARTISTS

Tim Bavington
Nick Cave
Subodh Gupta
Todd Hebert
Nir Hod
Barti Kher
Kerry James Marshall
Zwelethu Mthethwa
Adi Nes
Jackie Nickerson
Odili Donald Odita
Ravinder Reddy
Claudette Schreuders
Jonathan Seliger
Hank Willis Thomas
Carlos Vega

ADDRESS

513 West 20th Street
New York, NY 10011
USA
T: +1.212.645.1701
F: +1.212.645.8316
info@jackshainman.com
www.jackshainman.com

STAFF

Jack Shainman, Director
Claude Simard, Director
Judy Sagal,
    Associate Director
Zuleika Milan, Assistant
    Director
Joshua Howard,
    Art Handler

left: Adi Nes, **Jacob and Esau**, 2006, c-print, 50 x 60 inches; 127 x 152.4 cm
right: Kerry James Marshall, **Vignette**, 2005, acrylic on plexiglas, 72 x 60 inches; 182.88 x 177.8 cm

Stuart Shave / Modern Art

LONDON

ARTISTS

Bas Jan Ader
David Altmejd
Kenneth Anger
Simon Bill
Tom Burr
Mat Collishaw
Nigel Cooke
Barnaby Furnas
Tim Gardner
Lothar Hempel
Brad Kahlhamer
Phillip Lai
Barry McGee
Jonathan Meese
Alan Michael
Matthew Monahan
Katy Moran

Clare E. Rojas
Eva Rothschild
Lara Schnitger
Collier Schorr
Steven Shearer
Ricky Swallow
Clare Woods

ADDRESS

10 Vyner Street
E2 9DG London
UNITED KINGDOM
T: +44.20.89880.7742
F: +44.20.89880.7743
info@stuartshavemodern
   art.com
www.stuartshavemodern
   art.com

STAFF

Stuart Shave, Owner
JiMi Lee, Director
Kirk McInroy, Manager
Nadia Gerazouni,
   Co-Ordinator
Ilsa Colsell,
   Press Officer/Assistant
   to Director

Katy Moran, **Captain Beaky and his Band II**, 2006, acrylic on canvas, 23 2/3 x 19 3/4 x 1 1/6 inches; 60 x 50 x 3 cm

Shugoarts

TOKYO

ARTISTS	ADDRESS	STAFF
Are You Meaning Company	5th Floor	Shugo Satani, Director
Candice Breitz	1-3-2 Kiyosumi	Kaori Hoya
Yukio Fujimoto	Koto	Takenori Ohchi
Carsten Höller	135-0024 Tokyo	Satoko Oe
Mitsuhiro Ikeda	JAPAN	Yoko Harada
Leiko Ikemura	T: +81.3.5621.6434	
Runa Islam	F: +81.3.5621.6435	
Masato Kobayashi	info@shugoarts.com	
Naofumi Maruyama	www.shugoarts.com	
Boris Mikhailov		
Ritsue Mishima		
Yasumasa Morimura		
Ylva Ogland		
SHIMABUKU		
Sislej Xhafa		
Tomoko Yoneda		

left: Mitsuhiro Ikeda, **Untitled**, 2005, mixed media on cotton, 68 1/2 x 63 inches; 174 x 160 cm
right: Tomoko Yoneda, **Lovers, Dunaujvaros (formerly Stalin City), Hungary**, 2004, C-Type print, 31 1/8 x 38 1/6 inches; 79 x 97 cm, edition of 10

ARTISTS

Uta Barth
Marcel Dzama
Mari Eastman
Federico Herrero
Kris Martin
Damien Roach
Jon Pylypchuk
DJ Simpson
Florian Slotawa
Michael van Ofen
Neal Tait

ADDRESS

Poststrasse 2 + 3
D-40213 Düsseldorf
GERMANY
T: +49.211.135667
F: +49.211.135668
post@sieshoeke.com
www.sieshoeke.com

STAFF

Nina Höke
Alexander Sies
Diana Hunnewinkel
Carla Orthen
Tine Lurati

Michael van Ofen, **Untitled**, 2006, oil on canvas, 16 x 14 2/3 inches; 43 x 37 cm

Fredric Snitzer Gallery   MIAMI

ARTISTS

Hernan Bas
Bhakti Baxter
Cooper
John Espinosa
Naomi Fisher
Jacin Giordano
Luis Gispert
Jiawe Hwang
Beatriz Monteavaro
Gean Moreno
Gavin Perry
Norberto Rodriguez
Diego Singh
Alex Sweet
Michael Vasquez

ADDRESS

2247 North West
1st Place
Miami, FL 33127
USA
T: +1.305.448.8976
F: +1.305.573.5810
info@snitzer.com
www.snitzer.com

STAFF

Fredric Snitzer
Richard Arregui
Roxana Bruno, Director

Naomi Fisher, **Ladies (6/6/06 12:17 AM)**, ink on vellum, 42 x 30 inches; 106.68 x 76.2 cm

Sommer Contemporary Art   TEL-AVIV

ARTISTS

Darren Almond
Yael Bartana
Boyan Lazanof
Rineke Dijkstra
Ofir Dor
Karl Haendel
Alona Harpaz
Michal Helfman
Itzik Livneh
Muntean/ Rosenblum
Ugo Rondinone
Wilhelm Sasnal
Yehudit Sasportas
Ahlam Shibli
Netally Schlosser
Sandra Scolnick
Efrat Shvily
Doron Solomons

Eliezer Sonnenschein
Wolfgang Tillmans
Sharon Ya'ari
Rona Yefman
Guy Zagursky
Arthur Zmievsky

ADDRESS

13 Rothschild Boulevard
66881 Tel-Aviv
ISRAEL
T: +972.3.516.64.00
F: +972.3.516.86.77
mail@sommergallery.com
www.sommergallery.com

STAFF

Irit Mayer-Sommer
Tamar Zagursky
Ronili Lustig

Boyan, **YSL**, 2006, oil on canvas

Michael Stevenson Gallery

CAPE TOWN

ARTISTS

Conrad Botes
Wim Botha
David Goldblatt
Nicholas Hlobo
Pieter Hugo
Churchill Madikida
Mustafa Maluka
Samson Mudzunga
Zanele Muholi
Hylton Nel
Tracy Payne
Deborah Poynton
Berni Searle
Doreen Southwood
Guy Tillim
Barthélémy Toguo

ADDRESS

Hill House, De Smidt Street
Green Point
8005 Cape Town
SOUTH AFRICA
T: +27.21.421.2575
F: +27.21.421.2578
info@michaelstevenson.com
www.michaelstevenson.com

STAFF

Michael Stevenson
Joost Bosland
Andrew de Conceicao
Sophie Perryer
Kathy Skead

Mustafa Maluka, **Don't stand me down**, 2006, oil on canvas, 72 x 52 3/8 inches; 183 x 133cm

Galerie Diana Stigter

AMSTERDAM

ARTISTS

Tariq Alvi
Tjebbe Beekman
Martha Colburn
Amie Dicke
Elspeth Diederix
Matias Faldbakken
Rezi van Lankveld
Alisa Margolis
Fortuyn O'Brien
Saskia Olde Wolbers
Jimmy Robert
Julika Rudelius
Maaike Schoorel
Dieuwke Spaans
Iris van Dongen
Roman Wolgin

ADDRESS

Elandsstraat 90
NL-1016SH Amsterdam
THE NETHERLANDS
T: +31.20.624.2361
F: +31.20.624.2362
mail@dianastigter.nl
www.dianastigter.nl

STAFF

Diana Stigter, Director
David van Doesburg,
    Director
Leen Bedaux, Assistant,
    Manon Braat, Assistant

Rezi van Lankveld, **Matador**, 2005, oil on board, 48 x 48 inches; 122 x 122 cm

ARTISTS

Chris Evans
Aurélien Froment
Ryan Gander
Claire Harvey
Dan Holdsworth
Pamela Rosenkranz
Matthew Smith
Bedwyr Williams
Roman Wolgin

ADDRESS

27 Hoxton Street
N1 6NH London
UNITED KINGDOM
T: +44.20.7729.8171
F: +44.20.7729.8171
info@storegallery.co.uk
www.storegallery.co.uk

STAFF

Louise Hayward, Director
Niru Ratnam, Director
Gemma Holt, Manager

Ryan Gander, **Sapling**, 2006, A sapling tree placed beside the original tree planted to commemorate the opening of Le Corbusier's Pavilion l'Esprit Nouveau, Bologna (Photo credit: Polly Braden)

Sutton Lane

LONDON

ARTISTS

Slawomir Elsner
Henriette Grahnert
Justin Lieberman
Camilla Løw
Yuri Masnyj
Toby Paterson
Sean Paul
Eileen Quinlan
Blake Rayne
Christoph Ruckhäberle
Reena Spaulings
Joanne Tatham & Tom O'Sullivan
Cheyney Thompson
Michael Wilkinson

ADDRESS

1 Sutton Lane
EC1M 5PU London
UNITED KINGDOM
T: +44.20.7253.8580
F: +44.20.7253.6580
info@suttonlane.com
www.suttonlane.com

STAFF

Sabine Spahn, Director

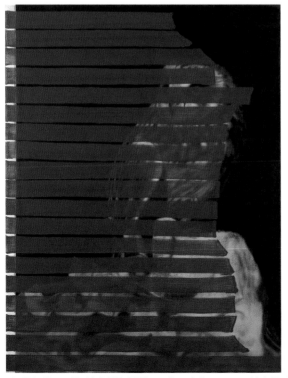 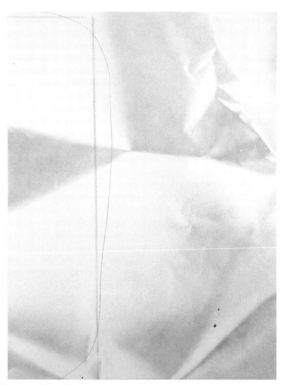

left: Blake Rayne, **Untitled #37**, 2006, acrylic and oil on canvas, 44 1/2 x 34 inches; 113 x 86.4 cm
right: Blake Rayne, **Untitled #32**, 2006, acrylic and oil on canvas, 44 1/2 x 34 inches; 113 x 86.4 cm

Taxter & Spengemann

NEW YORK

ARTISTS

Wayne Atkins
Lutz Bacher
Charlotte Becket
Frank Benson
Matt Calderwood
Xavier Cha
Devon Costello
Nancy de Holl
Lars Fisk
Matt Johnson
Corin Hewitt
Jaya Howey
Daniel Lefcourt
Scott Lenhardt
Kalup Linzy
Wardell Milan
Adam Putnam

Anna Schachte
Max Schumann
Macrae Semans

ADDRESS

504 West 22nd Street
New York, NY 10011
USA
T: +1.212.924.0212
F: +1.212.352.3540
info@taxterandspeng
   mann.com
www.taxterandspenge
   mann.com

STAFF

Kelly Taxter
Pascal Spengemann
Amy Mackie
Margot Norton

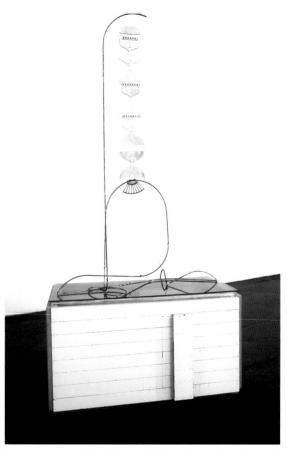

Macrae Semans, **Untitled (La Brea)**, 2005, wood, steel, glass, fabric, wicker, 75 x 38 x 20 inches; 190.5 x 96.52 x 50.8 cm

Richard Patterson, **Drawings from Dallas, no. 1**, 2005, [detail], mixed media on Hahnemuhle paper in 6 parts, framed dimensions: 17 1/2 x 13 1/4 inches; 44 x 34 cm

Team Gallery

NEW YORK

ARTISTS

Cory Arcangel
Pierre Bismuth
Slater Bradley
Brice Dellsperger
Gardar Eide Einarsson
Ross Knight
Jakob Kolding
Maria Marshall
Ryan McGinley
Dawn Mellor
Muntean/Rosenblum
Guillaume Pinard
Tam Ochiai
the estate of Steven Parrino
David Ratcliff
Jon Routson

Lisa Ruyter
Gert & Uwe Tobias
Banks Violette

ADDRESS

83 Grand Street
New York, NY 10013
USA
T: +1.212.279.9219
F: +1.212.279.9220
office@teamgal.com
www.teamgallery.com

STAFF

Jose Freire
Miriam Katzeff
Owen Clements
Scott Penkava

Slater Bradley, **Natalie Curtis, Manchester, 6/6/06**, 2006, C-print, 40 x 30 inches; 101.6 x 76,2 cm

Richard Telles Fine Art

LOS ANGELES

ARTISTS

Tom Allen
Roy Arden
Morika Baer
Ginny Bishton
Lecia Dole-Recio
Thomas Eggerer
Taft Green
Nathan Hylden
Rachel Harrison
Richard Hawkins
Jim Isermann
Michael Krebber
Lisa Lapinski
John Miller
Mathias Paledna
John Stezaker
Catherine Sullivan

ADDRESS

7380 Beverly Boulevard
Los Angeles, CA 90036
USA
T: +1.323.965.5578
F: +1.323.965.5579
tellesfineart@earthlink.net
www.tellesfineart.com

STAFF

Richard Telles, Director
Gladys Hernando,
    Assistant Director

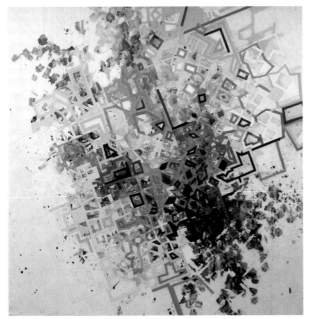

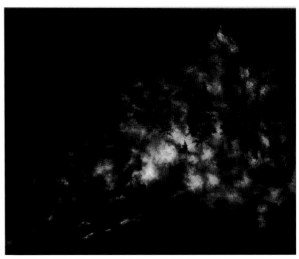

left: Lecia Dole-Recio, **Untitled**, 2006, gouache, graphite, tape, glue, paper, cardboard & vellum, 93 1/4 x 90 1/2 inches; 236.85 x 229.87 cm
right: Tom Allen, **Night of Fire**, 2006, oil on linen, 36 x 44 inches; 91.44 x 111.76 cm

Galerie Barbara Thumm

BERLIN

ARTISTS

Carlos Amorales
Fiona Banner
Bigert & Bergström
Sebastiaan Bremer
Fernando Bryce
Martin Dammann
Christian Hoischen
Sabine Hornig
Teresa Hubbard &
    Alexander Birchler
Alex Katz
Anne-Mie van Kerckhoven
Elke Krystufek
Johnny Miller
Mariele Neudecker
Julian Opie

Chloe Piene
Ann-Sofi Sidén
Heidi Specker

ADDRESS

Dircksenstrasse 41
D-10178 Berlin
GERMANY
T: +49.30.283.903.47
F: +49.30.283.904.57
info@bthumm.de
www.bthumm.de

STAFF

Barbara Thumm,
    Owner/Director
Ute Proellochs, Director

Chloe Piene, **Sign**, 2006, charcoal on vellum, 48 1/2 x 32 1/2 inches; 123.2 x 82.6 cm

Vilma Gold

ARTISTS

Dan Attoe
Nicholas Byrne
Alexandre da Cunha
William Daniels
Vladimir Dubossarsky &
  Aleksander Vinogradov
Brock Enright
Brian Griffiths
Daniel Guzman
Sophie von Hellermann
hobbypopMUSEUM
Thomas Hylander
Dani Jakob
Andrew Mania
Alisa Margolis

Aïda Ruilova
Michael Stevenson
Josef Strau
Mark Titchner

ADDRESS

25b Vyner Street
E2 9DG London
UNITED KINGDOM
T: +44.20.898.1334.4
F: +44.20.898.1335.5
mail@vilmagold.com
www.vilmagold.com

STAFF

Rachel Williams,
  Owner / Director
Sarah McCrory,
  Assistant Director
Chelsea Zaharczuk
Laurence Taylor

Nick Byrne, **Untitled (clown)**, 2006, oil on linen, 11 13/16 x 7 7/8 inches; 30 x 20 cm

Wallspace   NEW YORK

ARTISTS

Walead Beshty
Jacob Dyrenforth
Shannon Ebner
Dave Miko
Brad Phillips
Laura Riboli
Kirsten Stoltmann
Helen Verhoeven
Simon Willems
Mark Wyse

ADDRESS

619 West 27th Street
New York, NY
USA
T: +1.212.594.9478
F: +1.212.594.9805
info@wallspacegallery.com
www.wallspacegallery.com

STAFF

Rosemary Brooks
Janine Foeller
Jane Hait

Shannon Ebner, **Sculptures Involuntaires**, 2006, C-print, 50 x 60 inches; 127 x 152.40 cm

Galerie Barbara Weiss

BERLIN

ARTISTS

Monika Baer	John Miller
Heike Baranowsky	Rebecca Morris
Thomas Bayrle	Mai-Thu Perret
Janet Cardiff & George	Jean Frédéric Schnyder
Bures Miller	Andreas Siekmann
Maria Eichhorn	Roman Signer
Nicole Eisenman	Erik Steinbrecher
Ayse Erkmen	Niele Toroni
Friederike Feldmann	Marijke van Warmerdam
Christine & Irene	
Hohenbüchler	
Laura Horelli	
Jonathan Horowitz	
Raoul De Keyser	
Boris Mikhailov	

ADDRESS

Zimmerstrasse 88-91
D-10117 Berlin
GERMANY
T: +49.30.26.24.284
F: +49.30.265.165.2
mail@galeriebarbara
  weiss.de
www.galeriebarbaraweiss.de

STAFF

Barbara Weiss
Peer Golo Willi
Birgit Szepanski

Mai-Thu Perret, **Apocalypse Ballet**, 2006, Installation view, Galerie Barbara Weiss

Galerie Jan Wentrup

BERLIN

ARTISTS

Pablo Alonso
Marten Frerichs
Axel Geis
Mathew Hale
Gregor Hildebrandt
Michael Kalki
Jen Ray
Wawrzyniec Tokarski

ADDRESS

Choriner Staße 3
D-10119 Berlin
GERMANY
T: +49.30.48493600
F: +49.30.48493601
mail@janwentrup.com
www.janwentrup.com

STAFF

Jan Wentrup
Eva Knels

Axel Geis, **Figuren vor Pfeiler**, 2006, oil on canvas, 125 1/6 x 100 inches; 318 x 254 cm

White Cube/Jay Jopling

LONDON

ARTISTS

Franz Ackermann
Darren Almond
Ellen Altfest
Miroslaw Balka
Candice Breitz
Koen van den Broek
Jake & Dinos Chapman
Chuck Close
Gregory Crewdson
Carroll Dunham
Tracey Emin
Katharina Fritsch
Gilbert & George
Antony Gormley
Andreas Gursky
Marcus Harvey
Mona Hatoum
Eberhard Havekost
Damien Hirst
Gary Hume
Runa Islam
Sergej Jensen

Mika Kato
Anselm Kiefer
Martin Kobe
Liza Lou
Josiah Mcelheny
Christian Marclay
Julie Mehretu
Harland Miller
Sarah Morris
Gabriel Orozco
Damián Ortega
Richard Phillips
Marc Quinn
Jessica Rankin
Doris Salcedo
Hiroshi Sugimoto
Neal Tait
Sam Taylor-Wood
Fred Tomaselli
Gavin Turk
Jeff Wall
Cerith Wyn Evans

ADDRESS

48 Hoxton Square
N1 6PB London
UNITED KINGDOM
T: +44.207.749.7450
F: +44.207.749.7460

25-26 Mason's Yard
Off Duke Street, St James'
SW1Y 6BU London
UNITED KINGDOM
T: +44.207.766.3550
enquiries@whitecube.com
www.whitecube.com

STAFF

Jay Jopling
Daniela Gareh
Alexandra Mollof
Alison Ward
Graham Steele
Suzanne Egeran

Tracey Emin, **Thinking about it**, 2006, acrylic on canvas, 21 9/16 x 23 9/16 inches; 54.7 x 59.8 cm

Jan Winkelmann / Berlin

ARTISTS

Matthew Brannon
BURGHARD
Stéphane Dafflon
Plamen Dejanoff
Carsten Fock
Katarina Löfström
Dennis Loesch
Tilo Schulz

ADDRESS

Brunnenstrasse 185
D-10119 Berlin
GERMANY
T: +49.30.28.09.38.99
F: +49.30.28.09.39.08
info@janwinkelmann.com
www.janwinkelmann.com

STAFF

Jan Winkelmann
Jasmin Jouhar
Florian Rehn

Covered Animal Dishes

Plate 76

Plate 77

75

Glassware advert, From the collection of Matthew Brannon

Hiromi Yoshii

ARTISTS	ADDRESS	STAFF
Assume Vivid Astro Focus	6F 1-3-2 Kiyosumi	Hiromi Yoshii,
Björn Dahlem	Koutou	Owner/ Director
Kent Henricksen	135-0024 Tokyo	Emi Takahashi
Christian Holstad	JAPAN	Rumi Okamoto
Keegan McHargue	T: +81.3.5620.0555	Hiroyuki Sato
Tracy Nakayama	F: +81.3.5620.0550	Akie Oike
Daniel Roth	info@hiromiyoshii.com	Shino Yoshii
Bill Saylor	www.hiromiyoshii.com	
Josh Smith		
Yoshitaka Azuma		
Enlightenment		
Koichi Enomoto		
Taro Izumi		
Takehito Koganezawa		
Keisuke Maeda		
Soshiro Matsubara		

Koichi Enomoto, **untitled**, 2006, watercolor on paper, 29 3/4 x 22 inches; 75.5 x 56 cm

Zeno X Gallery

ANTWERP

ARTISTS

Michaël Borremans
Dirk Braeckman
Miriam Cahn
Anton Corbijn
Raoul De Keyser
Jan De Maesschalck
Stan Douglas
Marlene Dumas
Kees Goudzwaard
Noritoshi Hirakawa
Yun-Fei Ji
Kim Jones
Johannes Kahrs
John Körmeling
Mark Manders
Jenny Scobel

Maria Serebriakova
Luc Tuymans
Patrick Van Caeckenbergh
Anne-Mie Van Kerckhoven
Cristof Yvoré

ADDRESS

Leopold de Waelplaats 16
B-2000 Antwerp
BELGIUM
T: +32.3.216.16.26
F: +32.3.216.09.92
info@zeno-x.com
www.zeno-x.com

Zeno X Storage
Appelstraat 39
B-2140 Antwerp
BELGIUM
T: +32.3.216.26.26
F: +32.3.216.09.92

STAFF

Frank Demaegd, Director
Koen Van den Brande,
   Assistant
Jelle Breynaert, Assistant,
Rose Van Doninck,
   Assistant

Jenny Scobel, **Covered in birds**, 2006, graphite and wax on gessoed wooden panel, 24 x 42 7/8 inches; 61 x 109 cm

David Zwirner

NEW YORK

ARTISTS

Tomma Abts
Francis Alÿs
Mamma Andersson
Michaël Borremans
Stan Douglas
Marcel Dzama
Isa Genzken
On Kawara
R. Crumb
Raoul de Keyser
Rachel Khedoori
Toba Khedoori
Estate of Gordon
 Matta-Clark
John McCracken
Jockum Nordström
Chris Ofili
Raymond Pettibon

Neo Rauch
Estate of Jason Rhoades
Daniel Richter
Michael S. Riedel
Thomas Ruff
Katy Schimert
Yutaka Sone
Diana Thater
Luc Tuymans
James Welling
Christopher Williams
Sue Williams
Lisa Yuskavage

ADDRESS

525 West 19th Street
New York, NY 10011
USA
T: +1.212.727.2070
F: +1.212.727.2072
information@david
 zwirner.com
www.davidzwirner.com

533 West 19th Street
New York, NY 10011
USA

STAFF

David Zwirner, President
Angela Choon, Partner
Bellatrix Hubert, Partner
Hanna Schouwink, Partner
Amy Baumann, Director
Amy Davila, Director
Daelyn Short,
 Sales Associate

R. Crumb, **Big Healthy Girl Enjoys Deep Penetration From the Rear**, 1998, ink on paper, 14 x 16 3/4 inches; 35.5 x 42.5 cm

ARTISTS SPACE

THE MISSION OF ARTISTS SPACE IS TO ENCOURAGE EXPERIMENTATION, DIVERSITY AND DIALOGUE IN CONTEMPORARY ARTS PRACTICE, PROVIDE AN EXHIBITION SPACE FOR NEW ART AND ARTISTS, AND FOSTER AN APPRECIATION FOR THE VITAL ROLE THAT ARTISTS PLAY IN OUR COMMUNITY.

LIMITED EDITIONS

Since Hans Namuth produced his photographic portfolio edition for the organization in 1973, over fifty contemporary artists have generously donated editions for publication in support of Artists Space's programs.

We are proud to announce Nathan Carter, Ryan Gander, and Amy Sillman as our 2007 editions artists. Works by over 30 artists are currently available for sale, including Janine Antoni, Carroll Dunham, Ann Hamilton, Jim Hodges, Annette Messager, Jason Middlebrook, Tony Oursler, Richard Prince, Cindy Sherman, Carrie Mae Weems, and Andrea Zittel.

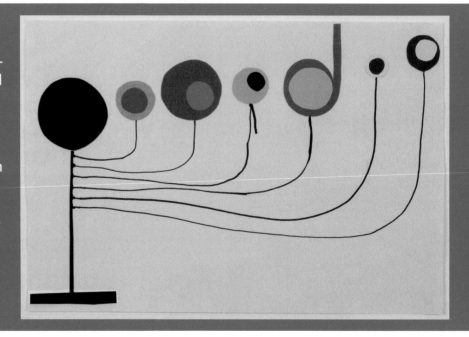

Nathan Carter
SOLAR-PLEX DRAWING, 2006,
Construction paper collage,
12.5 x 18.5 inches

38 GREENE STREET, 3RD FLOOR NEW YORK, NY 10013 PHONE: 212.226.3970 x 305 FAX: 212.966.1434
EDITIONS EMAIL: SHOWE@ARTISTSSPACE.ORG WWW.ARTISTSSPACE.ORG

Free Fish:
The Art of Yuken Teruya

THROUGH APRIL 29, 2007

He's been cutting up discarded fast food bags.
See what happens when he gets his hands on
Asia Society's Rockefeller Collection.

 **Asia**
Society

Asia Society and Museum 725 Park Avenue at 70th Street, NYC www.AsiaSociety.org • 212.517.ASIA

Yuken Teruya; *Happy Meal Crossing (Japan 2)* (detail); 2005; Paper and glue; 3 5/8 x 6 x 11 1/4 inches; Private Collection, New York, NY; Photograph courtesy of Josee Bienvenu Gallery

Access over 17,000 items on contemporary Asian art with one click.

Visit our website to access the online catalogue of over 17,000 items of material relating to contemporary Asian art from our collection, or search the up to-date World Events Calendar to find out what is happening around the globe.

More than a physical and on-line resource, the Asia Art Archive (AAA) plays an active role in organising programmes to encourage research and dialogue in the field. For more information on our new home and latest projects please visit our website **www.aaa.org.hk**

Asia Art Archive, 11/F, 233 Hollywood Road, Hong Kong
Tel: 2815-1112   Fax: 2815-0032   Email: info@aaa.org.hk

AAA is a registered charity in Hong Kong supported by the HKADC, private corporations, foundations, individuals, galleries and artists. For more information on our membership programmes please see our website

香港藝術發展局
Hong Kong Arts Development Council

AAA is financially supported by ADC

AIXI 27

APRIL 1 - JULY 29, 2007

OPENING RECEPTION SUNDAY, APRIL 1, 2 - 6 PM

BAMI ADEDOYIN BECCA ALBEE FANNY ALLIÉ JESSE ALPERN DORTHE ALSTRUP GABRIELA ALVA CAL Y MAYOR
JILL AUCKENTHALER GAIL BIEDERMAN HECTOR CANONGE CHRISTINE CATSIFAS JILLIAN CONRAD VINCE CONTARINO
JON CUYSON CAROLINE FALBY TRACEY GOODMAN PATRICK GRENIER EMILY HALL JOSEPH HART KETTA IOANNIDOU
ELAINE KAUFMANN JAYSON KEELING TAESEONG KIM JOSEPH MAIDA AMANDA MATHIS AMANDA MATLES MEGAN MICHALAK
HIROYUKI NAKAMURA ALISON OWEN CHIHCHENG PENG DAVID POLITZER EMILY PUTHOFF JENNA RANSOM
RASHANNA RASHIED-WALKER JASON REPPERT JOSEPH TEKIPPE WILL WALKER

THE BRONX MUSEUM OF THE ARTS 1040 GRAND CONCOURSE BRONX NY 10456-3999

WWW.BRONXMUSEUM.ORG **BRONXMUSEUM**

ARTIST IN THE MARKETPLACE (AIM) IS GENEROUSLY SUPPORTED BY THE JACQUES AND NATASHA GELMAN TRUST AND THE HELENA RUBINSTEIN FOUNDATION.
THE BRONX MUSEUM OF THE ARTS RECEIVES ONGOING GENERAL OPERATING SUPPORT FROM THE NEW YORK CITY DEPARTMENT OF CULTURAL AFFAIRS
WITH THE COOPERATION OF THE BRONX BOROUGH PRESIDENT ADOLFO CARRIÓN, JR. AND THE BRONX DELEGATION OF THE NEW YORK CITY COUNCIL,
NEW YORK STATE COUNCIL ON THE ARTS, BRONX DELEGATION OF THE NEW YORK STATE ASSEMBLY, U.S. SMALL BUSINESS ADMINISTRATION,
AND FROM PRIVATE SOURCES.

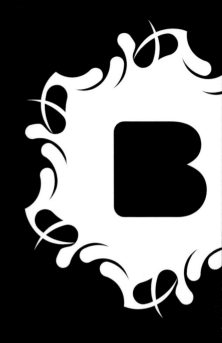

The Dinner Party Comes Home

Global Feminisms opens new Elizabeth A. Sackler Center for Feminist Art

MARCH 23, 2007 THROUGH JULY 15, 2007

Judy Chicago's iconic feminist masterpiece *The Dinner Party* will be a permanent installation in the new Elizabeth A. Sackler Center for Feminist Art, scheduled to open March 23, 2007. This dazzling new center dedicated to feminist art will open with *Global Feminisms*, a major international exhibition, featuring more than one hundred artists from over fifty countries.

Global Feminisms is made possible through the generous support of

Altria

Brooklyn Museum
www.brooklynmuseum.org

The Dinner Party, 1979. Brooklyn Museum Collection. A gift of the Elizabeth A. Sackler Foundation. (Detail.) Photograph by Donald Woodman.

Dia:Beacon
Riggio Galleries

A museum for Dia Art Foundation's renowned collection
of art from the 1960s to the present

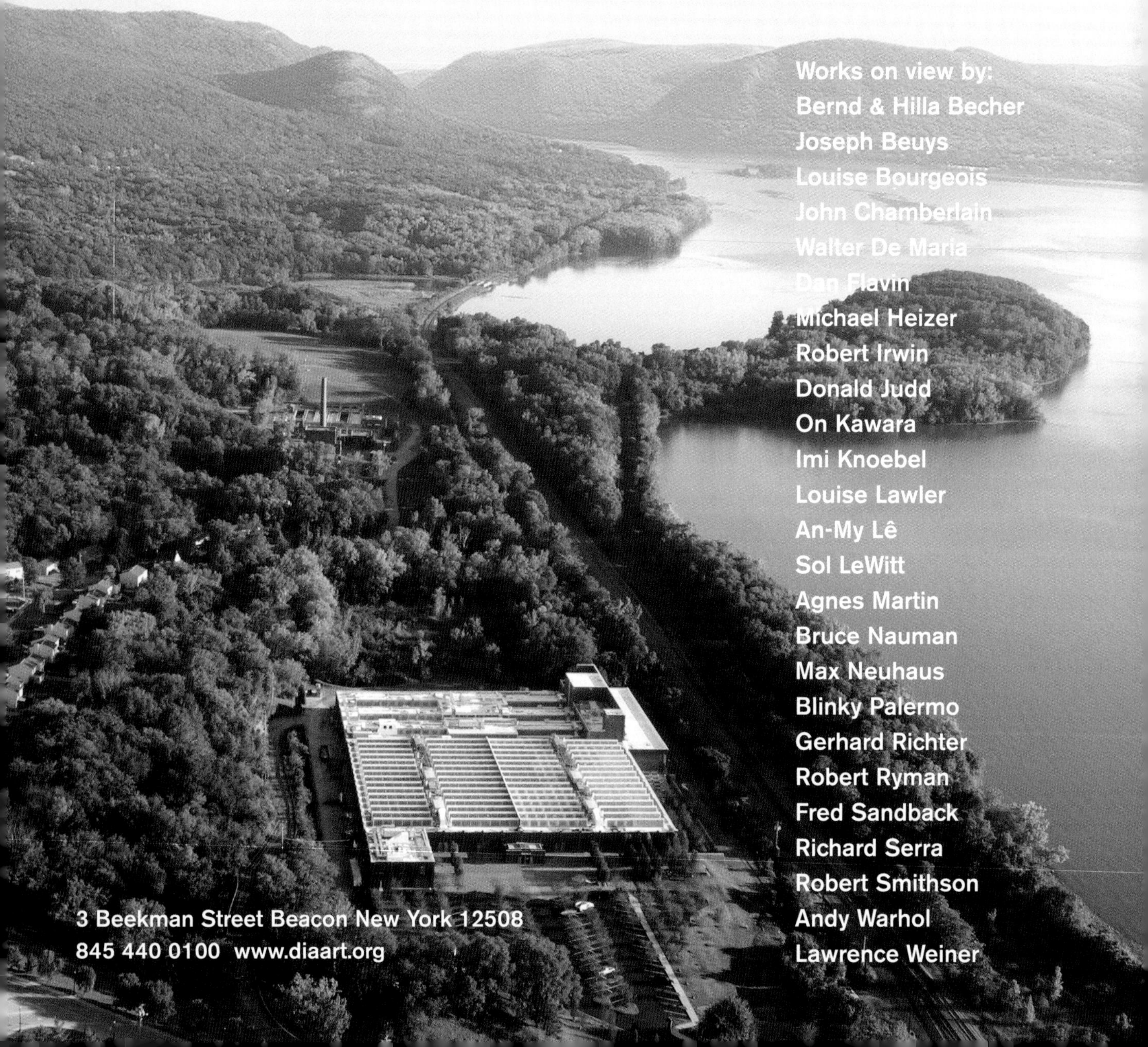

Works on view by:
Bernd & Hilla Becher
Joseph Beuys
Louise Bourgeois
John Chamberlain
Walter De Maria
Dan Flavin
Michael Heizer
Robert Irwin
Donald Judd
On Kawara
Imi Knoebel
Louise Lawler
An-My Lê
Sol LeWitt
Agnes Martin
Bruce Nauman
Max Neuhaus
Blinky Palermo
Gerhard Richter
Robert Ryman
Fred Sandback
Richard Serra
Robert Smithson
Andy Warhol
Lawrence Weiner

3 Beekman Street Beacon New York 12508
845 440 0100 www.diaart.org

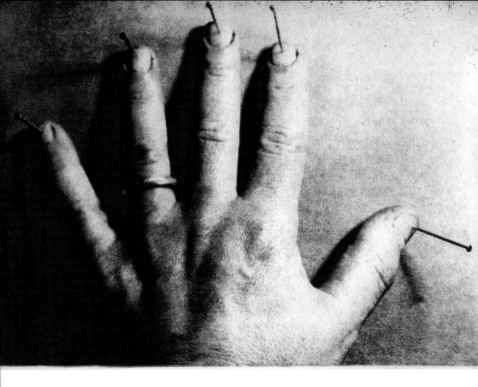

He practiced every day.

Luis Camnitzer, *From the Uruguayan Torture Series.* Suite of 35 four-color photo etchings, each 29.5 x 22 inches

THE DISAPPEARED
FEBRUARY 23 - JUNE 17, 2007

EL MUSEO DEL BARRIO
1230 FIFTH AVENUE AT 104TH STREET
NEW YORK, NY 10029
212 831 7272 WWW.ELMUSEO.ORG
WEDNESDAY - SUNDAY 11 - 5

El Greco to Picasso

Through March 28

GuggenheimMUSEUM

 Co-organized by

State Corporation for Spanish
Cultural Action Abroad

Media partner Thirteen / WNET

5th Ave at 89th St
Information 212 423 3500

Sat – Wed 10am – 5:45pm
Fri 10am – 7:45pm

Buy Advance Tickets at
guggenheim.org/picasso

International Center of Photography

HENRI CARTIER-BRESSON'S
SCRAPBOOK:
PHOTOGRAPHS, 1932–46

MARTIN MUNKÁCSI:
THINK WHILE YOU SHOOT!

LOUISE BROOKS
AND THE "NEW WOMAN"
IN WEIMAR CINEMA

January 19 – April 29, 2007

1133 Avenue of the Americas at 43rd Street   212.857.0000   www.icp.org

Jeff Wall

FEBRUARY 25–MAY 14, 2007

The exhibition is organized by The Museum of Modern Art and the San Francisco Museum of Modern Art. The New York presentation of the exhibition is made possible by Maja Oeri and Hans Bodenmann. The accompanying publications are made possible by Carol and David Appel.

Only at MoMA

11 W. 53 St. (212) 708-9400 MoMA.org

Jeff Wall. **Milk**. 1984. Silver dye bleach transparency (Cibachrome); aluminum light box. The Museum of Modern Art, New York. Acquired through the Mary Joy Thomson Legacy. © 2006 Jeff Wall

NEW

NEW MUSEUM STORE

MUSEUM

WWW.NEWMUSEUM.ORG

Free admission for VIP cardholders

plus a 10% discount on shop merchandise

NOW ON VIEW AT P.S.1

P.S.1 MoMA

CONTEMPORARY ART CENTER

22-25 JACKSON AVE. AT 46 AVE.
LONG ISLAND CITY
(718) 784-2084 WWW.PS1.ORG

EXHIBITIONS AT P.S.1 ARE MADE POSSIBLE BY
THE ANNUAL EXHIBITION FUND.

**VIK MUNIZ,
TOM SANDBERG,
NOT FOR SALE,
AND EMERGENCY
ROOM**

ABBAS KIAROSTAMI: IMAGE MAKER OPENS AT
P.S.1 AND THE MUSEUM OF MODERN ART ON
MARCH 1, 2007.

P.S.1 WELCOMES **THE ARMORY SHOW VIP CARD
HOLDERS** TO ATTEND SPECIAL ARTIST GALLERY
TALKS AT P.S.1 ON SATURDAY, FEBRUARY 24,
FROM 11:00 A.M. TO 1:00 P.M.

VIK MUNIZ, AKTE WEIMAR #157, 2006

Public Art Fund

One East 53rd Street, New York, NY 10022   212.980.4575   **www.publicartfund.org**

"WE ARE REBUILDING NEW YORK, NOT DISPERSING AND ABANDONING IT."

-Robert Moses

Robert Moses and the Modern City

On View Now

Three New York City venues examine the ambitious projects spearheaded by Robert Moses and view his legacy within the context of contemporary New York. Never-before-exhibited models, historic objects, plans, and vintage and new photography are featured, including a series by acclaimed photographer Andrew Moore, artist-in-residence at Dartmouth College.

QMA
QUEENS MUSEUM OF ART

MUSEUM OF THE CITY OF NEW YORK

MIRIAM & IRA D. WALLACH ART GALLERY

On view at
SculptureCenter
through
March 25, 2007
Monica Bonvicini

In Practice Project Series:
Alex Arcadia, Fia Backström,
Gardar Eide Einarsson,
The Manhattan Group
(Ross Cisneros and Garrett Ricciardi),
Amy O'Neill, Lucy Raven,
Karin Schneider,
Karen Yasinsky

SculptureCenter
44-19 Purves Street
Long Island City, New York 11101
t 718.361.1750
f 718.786.9336
www.sculpture-center.org
Thursday–Monday, 11am–6pm

Armory 2007 VIP pass holders and
exhibitors are entitled to free admission.

Limited Editions available at SculptureCenter

Peter Coffin
Untitled (Piano, Fruits and Vegetables) (detail)
2006
Thirteen 4 x 6" photographs, uncut and folded.
This sculpture is accompanied by a hand bound storage box.
Box dimensions: 16 x 16 x 4 1/2"
Edition of 20 with 3 artist proofs

Do-Ho Suh
Doorknob/Bathroom
2003
Polyester fabric, lithograph on paper in acrylic box.
7 3/4 x 12 x 18"
Edition of 20 with 3 artist proofs

Julianne Swartz
Clear Sky (detail)
2005
Concrete, stainless steel, silver.
8 x 5" base; 55" high
Edition of 25 with 3 artist proofs

Fred Wilson
Drop, Dripped
2003
Black and white glass.
"Drip": 3 1/2 x 15";
"Drop": 3 x 12"*
Edition of 20 with 3 artist proofs
*each piece is hand-blown; dimensions may vary slightly

Please call 718.361.1750 for pricing and more information.

SOCRATES SCULPTURE PARK

Long Island City, New York

www.socratessculpturepark.org

 socrates sculpture park

city of new york parks & recreation

Africa Comics
November 15, 2006 – March 18, 2007
The first US exhibition of
comic art from Africa

Also on view:
Stan Douglas:
Inconsolable Memories

Harlem Postcards
Featuring James Casebere,
Dominic McGill, Jessica Rankin
and Katy Schimert

More-in-Store
Harlem Toile de Jouy by Sheila Bridges
for Studio Printworks

StudioSound
Afrikya Volume 1: A Musical Journey
through Africa by Marcus Samuelsson
& Donna D'Cruz

The Studio Museum in Harlem
144 West 125th Street
New York, NY 10027
(212) 864-4500
studiomuseum.org

Mendozza y Caramba, *AAAAA!*, c. 2002 (detail), Courtesy of the artist and Africa e Mediterraneo, Bologna.

white columns

est. 1970

WHITECOLUMNS.ORG

TERENCE KOH

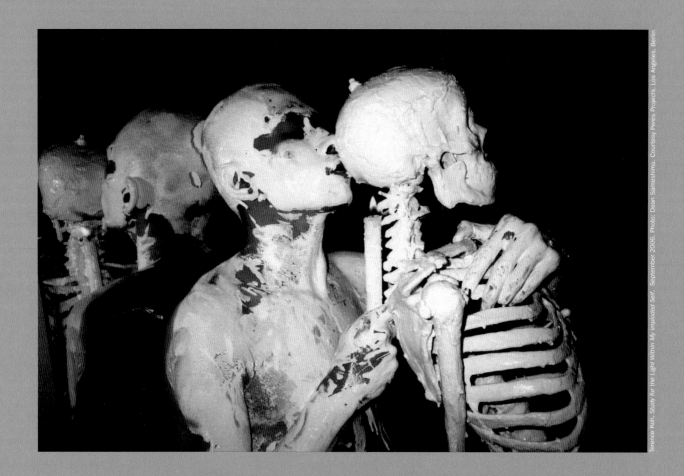

Terence Koh. *Study for the Light Within My Imploded Self*. September 2006. Photo: Dean Sameshima. Courtesy Peres Projects, Los Angeles, Berlin

Opening January 19

ALSO ON VIEW: | **GORDON MATTA-CLARK "YOU ARE THE MEASURE"** Opening February 22 | **LORNA SIMPSON** Opening March 1

WHITNEY

Whitney Museum of American Art · 945 Madison Avenue at 75th Street · 1(800) WHITNEY www.whitney.or

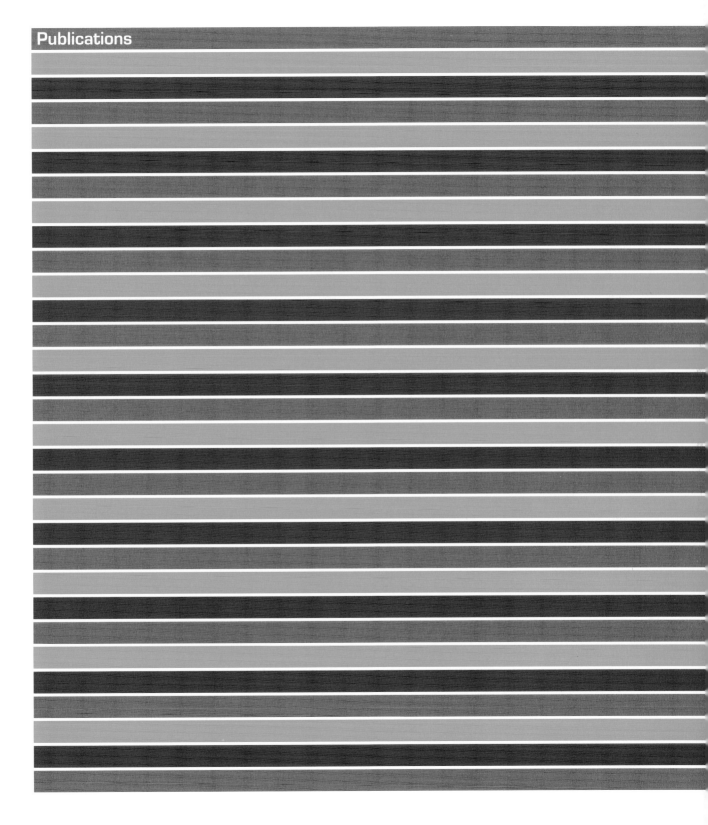

Publications

Art + Auction
111 8th Avenue, Suite 302
New York, NY 10011
USA
T 212.447.9555
www.artinfo.com

Art AsiaPacific
245 Eighth Avenue, #247
New York, NY 10011
USA
T 212.255.6003
www.aapmag.com

Art in America
575 Broadway, 5th Floor
New York, NY 10014
USA
T 212.941.2895
www.artinamericamagazine.com

Art Monthly
4th Floor, 28 Charing Cross Road
London WC2H 0DB
UNITED KINGDOM
T 44.0.207.240.0389
www.artmonthly.co.uk

Art Newspaper
594 Broadway, Suite 406
New York, NY 10012
USA
T 212.343.0727
www.theartnewspaper.com

Art on Paper Magazine
c/o Darte Publishing LLC
150 West 28th Street, Suite 504
New York, NY 10001
USA
T 212.675.1968
www.artonpaper.com

Art Papers
P.O. Box 5748
Atlanta, GA 31107
USA
T 404.588.1837
www.artpapers.org

art.es
Caracas 15, 7º
E-28010 Madrid
SPAIN
T 34.639.43.16.88
www.art-es.es

ArtChronika
18/1 Tverskaya Street, Office 802
127994 Moscow
RUSSIA
T 7.495.699.7023
www.artchronika.ru

Arte al Día
2150 Coral Way, Sixth Floor
Miami, FL 33145
USA
T 305.854.3050
www.artealdia.com

Arte y Parte - Revista de Arte
Tres de Noviembre, 31
39010 Santander/Cantabria
SPAIN
T 34.942.37.31.31
www.arteyparte.com

ARTFORUM International
350 Seventh Avenue, 19th Floor
New York, NY 10001
USA
T 212.475.4000
www.artforum.com

artinfo.com
111 8th Avenue, Suite 302
New York, NY 10011
USA
T 212.447.9555
www.artinfo.com

Artnet Worldwide
61 Broadway, 23rd Floor
New York, NY 10006
USA
T 212.497.9700
www.artnet.com

Artnet AG
Mauerstr. 83/84
D-10117 Berlin
GERMANY
T 49 (0) 30.20.91.780
www.artnet.de

ArtNexus
12955 Biscayne Blvd, Suite 410
Miami, FL 33181
USA
T 305.891.7270
www.artnexus.com

ArtNotes
Ciudad del Transporte
1-1 Pol. Industrial del Tambre
Santiago de Compostela (Coruña)
15890
SPAIN
T 34.981.575.804
www.artnotes.info

ArtPremium
1452 Ashford Avenue, Suite 306A
San Juan, PR 907
USA
T 787.721.6021
www.artpremium.com

Bidoun Magazine
195 Chrystie Street, Suite 600F
New York, NY 10002
USA
T 212.475.0123
www.bidoun.com

Blind Spot
210 Eleventh Avenue, Tenth Floor
New York, NY 10001
USA
T 212.633.1317
www.blindspot.com

Bomb Magazine
80 Hanson Place, #703
Brooklyn, NY 11217
USA
T 718.636.9100
www.bombsite.com

C Magazine
401 Richmond Street West, Suite 361
Toronto ON M5V 3A8
CANADA
T 416.539.9495
www.cmagazine.com

Camera Austria
Kunsthaus Graz Lendkai 1
A-8010 Graz
AUSTRIA
T 43.316.81.55.500
www.camera-austria.at

Circa
43/44 Temple Bar
Dublin 2
IRELAND
T 353.1.679.7388
www.recirca.com

Contemporary
K101 Tower Bridge Business Complex
100 Clements Road
London SE16 4DG
UNITED KINGDOM
T 44.207.740.1704
www.contemporary-magazine.com

Culture & Travel
111 8th Avenue, Suite 302
New York, NY 10011
USA
T 212.447.9555
www.artinfo.com

Eastern Art Report
P.O. Box 13666
London SW14 8WF
UNITED KINGDOM
T 44.208.392.1122
www.eapgroup.com

etc.
1-14-205 Kandajimbocho
Chiyoda Tokyo 101-0051
JAPAN
T 81.3.3292.9229
www.kotomizpress.jp

Eyeline
c/- Visual Arts QUT
Victoria Park Road Kelvin Grove, QLD
Queensland 4059
AUSTRALIA
T 61.7.38.64.55.20
www.qut.edu.au/eyeline/

Flash Art
799 Broadway, Suite 226
New York, NY 10003
USA
T 212.477.4905
www.flashartonline.com

Gallery Guide
111 8th Avenue, Suite 302
New York, NY 10011
USA
T 212.447.9555
www.artinfo.com

Map Magazine
14 High Street
Edinburgh EH1 1TE
UNITED KINGDOM
T 44.131.550.3095
www.mapmagazine.co.uk

Me Magazine
126 Winding Ridge Road
White Plains, NY 10603
USA
T 914.761.1860
www.memagazinenyc.com

Modern Painters
111 8th Avenue, Suite 302
New York, NY 10011
USA
T 212.447.9555
www.artinfo.com

Museums New York
111 8th Avenue, Suite 302
New York, NY 10011
USA
T 212.447.9555
www.artinfo.com

New Criterion
900 Broadway, Suite 602
New York, NY 10003
USA
T 212.247.6980
www.newcriterion.com

Parachute
4060, boul. Saint Laurent, #501
Montréal Quebec H2W 1Y9
CANADA
T 514.842.9805
www.parachute.ca

PerformArts
64 Boulevard Risso
BP 416906303
Nice Cedex 4
FRANCE
T 33.0.497.12.12.97
www.performarts.net

Photography Now
Chausseestrasse 16
D-10115 Berlin
GERMANY
T 49.30.2434.2780
www.photography-now.com

Prophecy Magazine
105 West 118th Street
New York, NY 10026
USA
T 347.220.1171
www.prophecymagazine.net

Revista Artmedia
Edificio Carisa, OF 2D
Los Yoses, San Jose
COSTA RICA
T 506.225.4301
www.artmediarevista.com

Segno
Corso Manthoné, 57
I-65127 Pescara
ITALY
T 39.085.61.438
www.fondazionesegno.it

Soma Magazine
888 O'Farrell Street, Suite 103
San Francisco, CA 94109
USA
T 415.777.4585
www.somamagazine.com

Spike
Sportmagazin Verlag GmbH
Heiligenstadter Lande 29
A-1190 Vienna
AUSTRIA
T 43 (0) 1.360.85.201
www.spikeart.at

Spot
Reforma #432 1er Piso
Juarez, México DF 6600
MEXICO
T 52.55.52.08.83.99
www.revistaspot.com

Springerin
Museumsplatz 1/Mezzanin
Fürstenhof
A-1070 Vienna
AUSTRIA
T 43.1.522.91.24
www.springerin.at

Studio Art Magazine
4 Ahuzat Bayit Street
Tel Aviv 61290
ISRAEL
T 972.3.516.5274
www.studiomagazine.co.il

Tema Celeste
Piazza Borromeo 10
20123 Milan
ITALY
T 39.02.8065.1794
www.temaceleste.com

Texte Zur Kunst
Torstraße 141
10119 Berlin
GERMANY
T 49.30.2804.7911
www.textezurkunst.de

**The International Guide to
Art Fairs and Antiques Shows**
799 Broadway
New York, NY 10003
USA
T 212.982.5429
www.artandantiquesfairguide.com

Uovo
Via Maria Vittoria 49
I-10123 Turin
ITALY
T 39.011.569.3876
www.uovo.it

Whitewall Magazine
135 William Street, #8B
New York, NY 10038
USA
T 646.649.3176
www.whitewallmag.com

Work. Art in Progress
Via Santa Chiara 30/F
I-10122 Turin
ITALY
T 39.011.436.71.97
www.hopefulmonster.net

Sixteen limited-edition, riverfront homes in The Chelsea Arts District

Architecture+interiors
by Annabelle Selldorf

200 Eleventh Avenue

www.200eleventh.com | +1 212 352 0222

Leonard Steinberg
Hervé Senequier
Prudential Douglas Elliman

THE INTERNATIONAL MAGAZINE FOR COLLECTORS

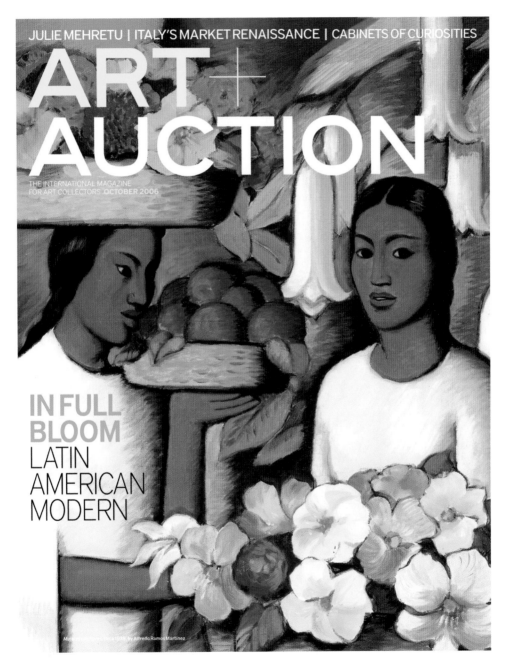

JULIE MEHRETU | ITALY'S MARKET RENAISSANCE | CABINETS OF CURIOSITIES

ART+
AUCTION

THE INTERNATIONAL MAGAZINE
FOR ART COLLECTORS ·OCTOBER 2006

IN FULL
BLOOM
LATIN
AMERICAN
MODERN

ArtAsiaPacific

TODAY'S ART FROM TOMORROW'S WORLD

ARTASIAPACIFIC IS THE LEADING AUTHORITY ON CONTEMPORARY ART FROM ASIA, THE PACIFIC AND THE ASIAN DIASPORA.

Highlighting emerging artists and providing in-depth analysis of the artists and art movements which shape the artistic scene today. Every issue is packed with insight, information and images from around the globe. *ArtAsiaPacific* is the most current and comprehensive magazine, giving you today's art from tomorrow's world.

SUBSCRIBE NOW
SUBSCRIBE@AAPMAG.COM

WWW.AAPMAG.COM

AMERICA'S MOST PRESTIGIOUS ART FAIR
THE 19TH ANNUAL ART SHOW TO BENEFIT

Henry Street Settlement

ORGANIZED BY THE

Art Dealers Association of America

FEBRUARY 22–26, 2007
GALA PREVIEW: WEDNESDAY FEBRUARY 21
PARK AVENUE AT 67TH STREET, NEW YORK CITY

ADAA

George Adams Gallery
Adler & Conkright Fine Art
Brooke Alexander/
    Brooke Alexander Editions
Ameringer & Yohe Fine Art
John Berggruen Gallery
Cheim & Read
Garth Clark Gallery
Conner-Rosenkranz LLC
CRG Gallery
D'Amelio Terras
Danese
DC Moore Gallery
Richard L. Feigen & Co.
Peter Findlay Gallery
Fischbach Gallery
Fraenkel Gallery
Peter Freeman, Inc.
Galerie St. Etienne
Gladstone Gallery
James Goodman Gallery
Marian Goodman Gallery
Richard Gray Gallery
Greenberg Van Doren Gallery
Lillian Heidenberg Fine Art
Rhona Hoffman Gallery
Edwynn Houk Gallery
Leonard Hutton Galleries
Paul Kasmin Gallery
Knoedler & Company
Barbara Krakow Gallery
Hans P. Kraus Jr.
    Fine Photographs
L&M Arts
Margo Leavin Gallery

Lehmann Maupin
Galerie Lelong
Lennon, Weinberg
Locks Gallery
Jeffrey H. Loria & Co., Inc.
L.A. Louver
Luhring Augustine
Matthew Marks Gallery
Mary-Anne Martin/Fine Art
Barbara Mathes Gallery
McKee Gallery
Anthony Meier Fine Arts
Robert Miller Gallery
Mitchell-Innes & Nash
Moeller Fine Art, Ltd.
Montgomery Gallery
Donald Morris Gallery, Inc.
David Nolan Gallery
Pace Prints
PaceWildenstein
Martha Parrish & James Reinish, Inc.
Andrea Rosen Gallery
Susan Sheehan Gallery
Sikkema Jenkins & Co.
Manny Silverman Gallery
Skarstedt Fine Art
Sonnabend Gallery
Sperone Westwater
Tasende Gallery
David Tunick, Inc.
Valley House Gallery Inc. &
    Sculpture Garden
Washburn Gallery
Michael Werner
Riva Yares Gallery
Donald Young Gallery
Zabriskie Gallery
David Zwirner Gallery

GALA TICKETS: 212.766.9200
FOR EXHIBITION INFORMATION: 212.940.8925
WWW.ARTDEALERS.ORG/ARTSHOW

LEAD UNDERWRITING GENEROUSLY PROVIDED BY
LEHMAN BROTHERS

Art in America

dada da dada dadadadadadada dada dada epep epep dada

E ach month *Art in America* brings you insightful commentary on major museum events, current exhibition reviews, revealing interviews, exciting new artists and news from around the world of art. There is simply no better source of information that covers the international art scene.

Subscribe: 800.925.8059 in the U.S. or call 515.242.0297 worldwide   **Advertise:** call 212.941.2854

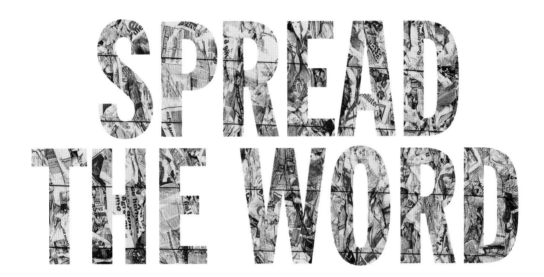

rt.es
ational_contemporary_art

art.es project #14: Nelson Leirner

www.art-es.es

Caracas 15, 7º
28010 Madrid. Spain.
contact@art-es.es

art.es Project / Proyecto art.es #14:

Nelson Leirner, *Erótico Klint y Leirner / Erotic Klint and Leirner (2006).*

every issue appears a Project produced by an international artist exclusively for art.es (cover + 12-14 pages). This makes the magazine a creative space and a collector's item.

Cada número publica un Proyecto hecho en exclusiva por un artista internacional para art.es (portada + 2-14 páginas). Esto hace de ella un espacio creativo y una revista de colección.

art.es
international_contemporary_art

+¡¡¡ *Be CreaCtive* !!!+
+¡¡¡ *Sé CreaCtivo* !!!+

Photo: Jessica Craig-Martin.

Have you SCENE & HERD?

Agenda-setting gossip since 2004.

www.artforum.com/diary

What's really happening in the art world?

artnet®

is it on artnet?

ArtNexus

magazine

artnexus.com

press releases

editions

ن و ب ي د BIDOUN
SPRING/SUMMER 2005
ARTS AND CULTURE FROM THE MIDDLE EAST

ن و ب ي د BIDOUN
WINTER 2005
ARTS AND CULTURE FROM THE MIDDLE EAST

ن و ب ي د BIDOUN
WINTER 2005
ARTS AND CULTURE FROM THE MIDDLE EAST

ن و ب ي د BIDOUN
FALL 2006
ARTS AND CULTURE FROM THE MIDDLE EAST

B دبي DUBAI 90990

WWW.BIDOUN.COM

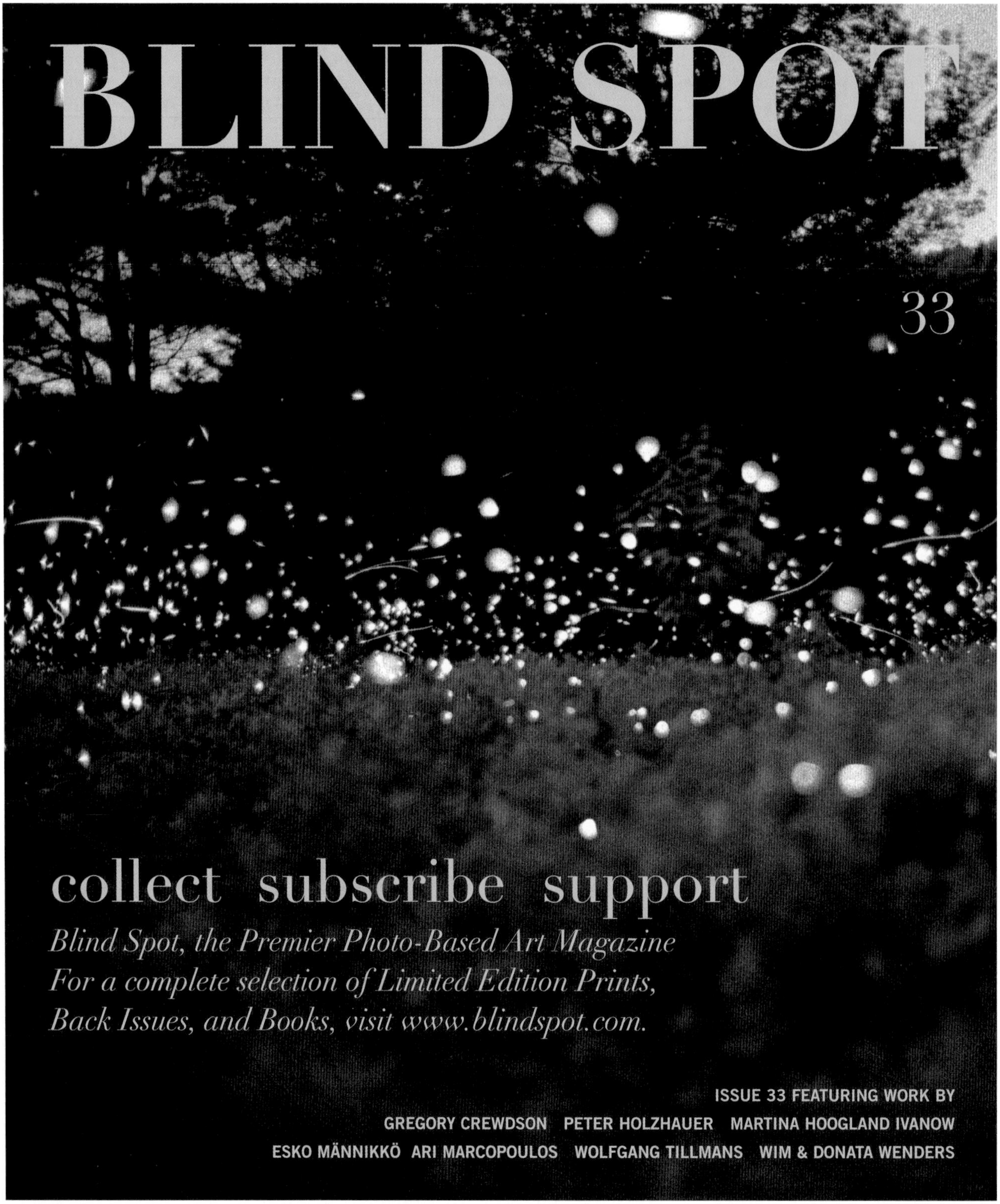

BLIND SPOT
33
collect subscribe support
Blind Spot, the Premier Photo-Based Art Magazine
For a complete selection of Limited Edition Prints,
Back Issues, and Books, visit www.blindspot.com.
ISSUE 33 FEATURING WORK BY
GREGORY CREWDSON PETER HOLZHAUER MARTINA HOOGLAND IVANOW
ESKO MÄNNIKKÖ ARI MARCOPOULOS WOLFGANG TILLMANS WIM & DONATA WENDERS

(cover image) Gregory Crewdson *Untitled*, 1996 from *Fireflies*

CEREALART

149 North 3rd Street
Philadelphia, PA 19106
www.cerealart.com

E info@cerealart.com
T 215.627.5060

Editions and multiples by:

Maurizio Cattelan
Phil Collins
Roberto Colugi
Elmgreen & Dragset
Marcel Dzama
Massimiliano Gioni
Keith Haring

Kirsten Hassenfeld
Yayoi Kusama
James Marshall
Walter Martin & Paloma Muñoz
Allan McCollum
Adam McEwen
Ryan McGinness
Keegan McHargue

Taylor McKimens
Yoshitomo Nara
Yoshua Okon
Elizabeth Peyton
Paola Pivi
Kenny Scharf
Shirana Shahbaz
Laurie Simmons

Andreas Slominski
Ali Subotnick
Momoyo Torimitsu
Lawrence Weiner
Kehinde Wiley
Tommy White

Walter Martin and Paloma Muñoz, *Traveler 186*, 2006, Edition of 250, hand signed, glass, resin, injection molded plastic, wood, water
globe diameter: 4.75 inches / 12.1cm, overall: 6 inches / 15.24cm

CEREALART Project Room: *Inky Toy,* curated by Anna-Catharina Gebbers, February 16 - April 14, 2007
Nicole Bianchet, Ulla von Brandenburg, Lucile Desamory, Claire Fontaine, Lisa Junghanss, Dorota Jurczak, Isa Melsheimer

contemporary 212121

Due to the success of our special issues which have focused on a number of different themes in the past, Such as 'painting', 'photography', 'curators' and 'collections', contemporary has now increased the number Of these special profiles issues, entitled contemporary21, from four to six each year to be published bi Monthly.

To order copies of contemporary 21 special issues call +44 (0)20 7740 1704 or email Subscribe@contemporary-magazine.com

Contemporary now publishes a special yearly issue. The first contemporary annual features 50 profiles on emerging artists from all over the world, selected from our global network of contributing editors.

THREE GREAT REASONS TO SUBSCRIBE

- save over 25% on cover price
- students save over 50%
- read us before we hit the news-stands
- free numbered and editioned artworks
  exclusive to contemporary subscribers

HOW TO SUBSCRIBE

- fax: +44 (0) 20 7252 3510
- email: subscribe@contemporary-magazine.com
- on-line: www.contemporary-magazine.com
- by post: return the subscription card
- enquiries: +44 (0) 020 7252 3998

contemporary annual

INSPIRATION FOR THE PASSIONATE TRAVELER

Culture & Travel

ROME:
The Birthplace
of Celebrity

IRELAND:
Holy Ruins and
Sacred Towers

CHICAGO:
Modernism
Faces
the Future

HYDRA:
Brice Marden's
Greek Island
Inspiration

CHINA:
A Provincial
City Goes
Avant-Garde

Premiere Issue
Sept/Oct 2006

Eastern Art
REPORT

Art and Artists from Iran

A SPECIAL PRESENTATION
EDITED BY SAJID RIZVI & SHIRLEY RIZVI

Table of Contents

East Asia Journal
STUDIES IN MATERIAL CULTURE

East Asia Journal: Studies in Material Culture takes an interdisciplinary approach to the study of material culture in East Asia — China, Japan and Korea — as well as the countries of the Southeast Asian region.

Authors in the latest issue include Gina Barnes, Chialing Yang, Lin Su Hsing and Delin Lai. Visit www.eapgroup.com/eaj0.htm for table of contents and ordering info

subscribe, make contact

Subscriptions
Eastern Art Publishing [EAP]
P O Box 13666, London SW14 8WF, United Kingdom
T +44-[0]20 8392 1122 | F +44-[0]20 8392 1422
E info@eapgroup.com| W www.eapgroup.com

Websites for the art world

www.exhibit-e.com

The World's Leading Art Magazine Vol. XXXIV No.250 October 2006 US $8.00 €7,00 International

Flash Art

Michaël Borremans
"Weight"
Video still

Art Diary 06/07
the world art directory
Those who look for you
look in Art Diary

The most widely-read, best informed, most controversial contemporay art magazine in the world today. *Flash Art*, described as the "reliable barometer of the *Zeitgeist*," has become an unrivaled reference point for artists, critics, art dealers, philosophers, and writers. *Flash Art* is there to keep you informed of what is really happening in the contemporary art world, because today's news is the history of our time.

Flash Art / Giancarlo Politi Editore
68, Via Carlo Farini - I-20159 - Milan
Tel. +39 02 68 87 341 Fax +39 02 66 80 12 90
www.flashartonline.com

Flash Art / U.S.
Kate Shanley, 799 Broadway,
Rm 226, New York NY 10003
Tel. +1 212 477 4905 Fax: +1 212 477 5016
flashartads@aol.com

MICHELANGELO PISTOLETTO

JAN FABRE

WHEN COFFEE BECOMES ART

THE ILLY COLLECTION WAS CREATED TO ENHANCE EVERY MOMENT SPENT DRINKING ILLY, THE WORLD'S FINEST ESPRESSO COFFEE. THROUGH AN ONGOING COMMITMENT TO THE ARTS, ILLY INVITES RENOWNED AND EMERGING ARTISTS TO LOOK UPON ITS CUPS AS EMPTY CANVASES. THE RESULT IS AN INSPIRING AND ECLECTIC REPERTOIRE OF ORIGINAL WORKS OF ART. TO VIEW OUR CURRENT SELECTION OF ARTIST CUPS, VISIT ILLYUSA.COM.

MICHAEL LIN

illy

SEPTEMBER 1, 2006– AUGUST 31, 2007

THE INTERNATIONAL GUIDE TO ART FAIRS AND ANTIQUES SHOWS

2006/2007 SEASON

Featuring the details on over 100 forthcoming major international events in 33 cities and 18 countries and including more than 70 two-page color presentations of leading shows and 150 color illustrations of artworks and objects to be offered at these events by some of the world's leading art and antiques dealers.

Subscribe now to receive the new annual edition for two years at only $12 per issue. You pay just $24* and you save $12.

To subscribe by Fax: +1 212 673 9507 or by email: artmediaco@aol.com

*$45 outside the United States

ART
MATTERS:

 tastic rooms

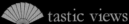 tastic views

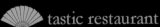 tastic restaurant

 tastic spa

The world's most luxurious hotel group in the world's most exciting city.

MANDARIN ORIENTAL
NEW YORK
SM

80 Columbus Circle at 60th Street, New York, NY 10023. For reservations, visit www.mandarinoriental.com or call toll free (866) 801 8880.

MODERNPAINTERS

The International Art Magazine
SEPTEMBER 2006

LONDON vs. NEW YORK
Which is Worse?

KIKI SMITH
Insides Out

PLUS
JERRY SALTZ
MATTHEW COLLINGS
VINCE ALETTI

BARNEY ON BEUYS

66 He remains a cornerstone of my faith that art provides useful tools for understanding the world that can proliferate into the broader culture. 99

THE SOURCE FOR ARTS LOVERS

MUSEUMS
NEW YORK

FALL 2006

Contemporary
Artists Reflect
on Slavery

At Home with Power Patron Beth Rudin DeWoody
Museums Tackle Antiquities Issues

ART+ MUSEUMS
MAGAZINES

VOLUME 12 NO. 4
MUSEUM LISTINGS AND
CALENDAR OF EVENTS

SUBSCRIBE: 1 800 710 9409

numéro 3 | 4€
Automne 2006

perform**Arts**

ARTVISUEL · **ART**VIVANT

perform**Arts**
ARTVISUEL · ARTVIVANT

Zoo | Bettina Rheims | Le festival d'Avignon | Chauffe Marcel ! | L'Objet du désir | Michel Butor | De l' Absurde au
Théâtre national de Nice | Do not disturb ! Art, provocation et engagement | Zaha Hadid & Frédéric Flamand |

M 02399 - 3 H - F: 4,00 €

Autriche : 4,7€ | Belgique : 4€ | Canada 6,95 CAD | Allemagne 4,7€ | DOM 4,7€
Italie : 4,7€ | Luxembourg : 4,7€ | Maroc : 52 mad. | Pays-Bas : 4,7€ | Portugal (cont) : 4,7€

www.perform**arts**.net

www.perform**arts**.net

e-news | calendar | archives
contemporary art at your fingertips

SMART.
PROVOCATIVE.
ESSENTIAL.

QUINTESSENTIALLY

Quintessentially - the world's leading private members' club and concierge service - is your vital link to the very best hotels, clubs, gyms, spas and restaurants across the globe. With access to the latest film premieres, charity events, gala balls, shopping evenings, VIP after-parties, concerts, festivals, theatre and sporting events, as well as fantastic wine club, a membership to Quintessentially keeps you on the inside track 24 hours a day, 365 days a year.

The Quintessentially Arts Club celebrates art and culture all over the world. Throughout the year and all over the globe, the Quintessentially Arts Club hold entertaining and high-quality events from across the spectrum of the arts, including a wide range of private views, specialist art talks, preview exhibitions and meet the artist evenings.

World: 1800 884 4797
www.quintessentially.com

LONDON | MANCHESTER | DUBLIN | CANNES | ISTANBUL | OSLO | HELSINKI | COPENHAGEN | STOCKHOLM | MOSCOW | NEW YORK | MIAMI
LOS ANGELES | HONG KONG | SHANGHAI | BANGKOK | DUBAI | BEIRUT | KUWAIT | SAUDI ARABIA | CAPE TOWN | JOHANNESBURG

spike

ART QUARTERLY

**The international
art magazine for
Central and Eastern
Europe**

www.spikeart.at

tema celeste

contemporaryart

117

sebastian diaz morales

NATURALLY

 vivavi

Contemporary Sustainable Furniture

Brooklyn Showroom   866.848.2840   www.vivavi.com

whitewall

THE UNSEEN WORLD OF CONTEMPORARY ART

SUBSCRIBE

THE UNSEEN WORLD OF
CONTEMPORARY ART

WWW.WHITEWALLMAG.COM

WPS1 MoMA

ART RADIO   **WPS1.ORG**

LIVE FROM THE ARMORY

ART RADIO WPS1.ORG IS THE OFFICIAL WEB RADIO STATION OF THE ARMORY SHOW 2007.

VISIT OUR BROADCAST BOOTH AND LISTEN TO LIVE ON-LOCATION INTERVIEWS FROM FRIDAY TO SUNDAY, FEBRUARY 23–25, FROM 2–5 P.M. EST

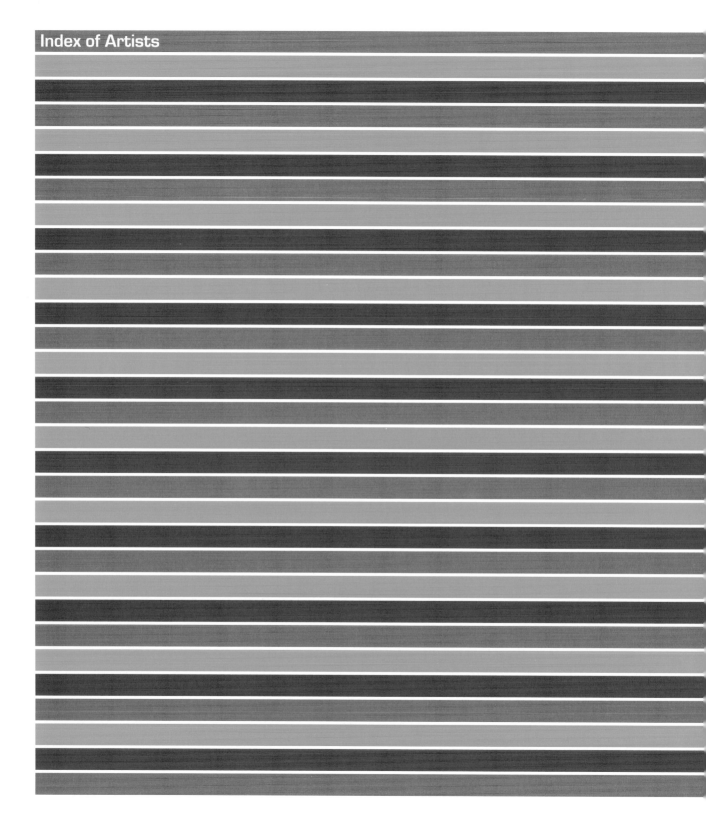

Index of Artists

Abdessemed, Adel
Galerie Kamel Mennour

Abramovic, Marina
Sean Kelly Gallery
Lia Rumma

Abts, Tomma
greengrassi
David Zwirner

Ackermann, Franz
Mai 36 Galerie
Meyer Riegger Galerie
White Cube/Jay Jopling

Ackermann, Rita
Annet Gelink Gallery
Galerie Almine Rech
Hotel

Acosta, Scoli
Daniel Reich Gallery

Adach, Adam
Arndt & Partner Berlin/Zurich
D'Amelio Terras

Adams, Robert
Matthew Marks Gallery

Adels, Simone
Angles Gallery

Adler, Amy
Galleria Massimo De Carlo
Taka Ishii Gallery

Ahn, Kyuchul
Arario Gallery

Aitchison, Craigie
Timothy Taylor Gallery

Aitken, Doug
303 Gallery
Galerie Eva Presenhuber
Taka Ishii Gallery
Victoria Miro Gallery

Akakce, Haluk
Galerist
COSMIC Galerie
The Approach

Akerman, Chantal
Frith Street Gallery

Albenda, Ricci
Andrew Kreps Gallery

Albers, Jan
Sara Meltzer Gallery

Albers, Josef
PaceWildenstein

Aldrich, Richard
Corvi-Mora
Marc Foxx

Alexander, Andy
China Art Objects

Alfred, Brian
Haunch of Venison

Ali, Laylah
303 Gallery

Allen, Phillip
Kerlin Gallery
The Approach

Allen, Tom
Richard Telles Fine Art

**Allora & Guillermo
Calzadilla Jennifer**
Galerie Chantal Crousel
Lisson Gallery

Almond, Darren
Galerie Chantal Crousel
Matthew Marks Gallery
White Cube/Jay Jopling

Alonso, Pablo
Galerie Jan Wentrup

Altfest, Ellen
Bellwether
White Cube/Jay Jopling

Althoff, Kai
Galerie Christian Nagel

Altmejd, David
Stuart Shave/Modern Art

Alvarez, Jose
Gavlak

Alvi, Tariq
Galerie Diana Stigter

Alÿs, Francis
David Zwirner
Yvon Lambert Paris/New York

Amer, Ghada
Kukje Gallery

Amm, Markus
David Kordansky Gallery
Herald St
The Breeder

Amorales, Carlos
Annet Gelink Gallery
Galerie Barbara Thumm
Yvon Lambert Paris/New York

Anderson, Alice
Yvon Lambert Paris/New York

Anderson, Hurvin
Thomas Dane Gallery

Anderson, Laurie
Sean Kelly Gallery

Andersson, Mamma
David Zwirner
Galleri Magnus Karlsson

Andersson, Roger
Galleri Magnus Karlsson
Sara Meltzer Gallery

**Andrade. Tudela
Armando**
Annet Gelink Gallery

Andre, Carl
Yvon Lambert Paris/New York

Anger, Kenneth
Stuart Shave/Modern Art

Auerbach, Lisa Anne
Gavlak

Antille, Emmanuelle
Galerie Eva Presenhuber

Antin, Eleanor
Ronald Feldman Fine Arts, Inc.

Antunes, Leonor
Dicksmith Gallery

Aoki, Ryoko
Kodama
Marc Foxx

Aoshima, Chiho
Blum & Poe
Galerie Emmanuel Perrotin

Apfelbaum, Polly
Angles Gallery
Frith Street Gallery

Appel, Kevin
Angles Gallery
Marianne Boesky Gallery

Applebroog, Ida
Ronald Feldman Fine Arts, Inc.

Araki, Nobuyoshi
Anton Kern Gallery
Galerie Almine Rech
Galerie Kamel Mennour
Taka Ishii Gallery

Aranberri, Ibon
Galeria Pepe Cobo

Arbus, Diane
Robert Miller Gallery

Arcangel (beige), Cory
Team Gallery

Arceneaux, Edgar
Adamski Gallery for
Contemporary Art
Galerie Praz-Delavallade

Arden, Roy
Richard Telles Fine Art

Ardouin, Pierre
Galerie Chez Valentin

**Are You Meaning
Company**
Shugoarts

Argianas, Athanasios
The Breeder

Arienti, Stefano
Lehmann Maupin

Armleder, John
Galleria Massimo De Carlo

Galerie Kamel Mennour
Matthew Marks Gallery

Arnaud, Pierre-Olivier
Art : Concept

Arrhenius, Lars
Galleri Magnus Karlsson

Arsham, Daniel
Galerie Emmanuel Perrotin

Art & Language
Lisson Gallery

Artschwager, Richard
David Nolan Gallery
Georg Kargl

Ashton Harris, Lyle
CRG Gallery

Askevold, David
CANADA

Assaël, Micol
Johann König

Assume Vivid Astro Focus
Hiromi Yoshii
John Connelly Presents
Peres Projects

Ataman, Kutlug
Lehmann Maupin

Atay, Fikret
Galerie Chantal Crousel

Atherton, Hope
Bortolami Dayan
Patrick Painter, Inc.

Atkins, Wayne
Taxter & Spengemann

Atkinson, Conrad
Ronald Feldman Fine Arts, Inc.

Attia, Kader
Andréhn-Schiptjenko
Galerie Christian Nagel

Attoe, Dan
Peres Projects
Vilma Gold

Audebert, Julien
Art : Concept

Auer, Abel
Corvi-Mora

Auerbach, Tauba
Deitch Projects

Avini, Andisheh
Gavlak

Avora, Emi
Greenberg Van Doren Gallery

Avotins, Janis
Johnen/Schöttle
IBID Projects

Azuma, Yoshitaka
Hiromi Yoshii

Bacher, Lutz
Taxter & Spengemann

Bader, Darren
Rivington Arms

Baechler, Donald
Cheim & Read
Galerie Thaddaeus Ropac

Baer, Monika
Galerie Barbara Weiss
Galerie Eva Presenhuber
Richard Telles Fine Art

Baghramian, Nairy
Galerie Christian Nagel

Baik, Hyunjin
Arario Gallery

Baker, Jimmy
Foxy Production

Baker, Kristin
Deitch Projects

Baldessari, John
Galeria Pepe Cobo
Mai 36 Galerie

de Balincourt, Jules
Arndt & Partner Berlin/Zurich
Zach Feuer Gallery

Balka, Miroslaw
White Cube/Jay Jopling

Balkenhol, Stephan
Johnen/Schöttle
Mai 36 Galerie
Galeria Pepe Cobo

Ballantyne, Chris
Peres Projects

Ballen, Roger
Galerie Kamel Mennour
Johnen/Schöttle

Balmet, Gilles
COSMIC Galerie

Bamber, Judie
Angles Gallery

Ban, Chinatsu
Marianne Boesky Gallery

Banhart, Devendra
CANADA

Banner, Fiona
Frith Street Gallery
Galerie Barbara Thumm

Baranowsky, Heike
Galerie Barbara Weiss

Barbeito, Pedro
Lehmann Maupin

Barbosa, Felipe
Sara Meltzer Gallery

Barcelo, Miquel
Timothy Taylor Gallery
Yvon Lambert Paris/New York

Bareikis, Aidas
Leo Koenig, Inc., Inc.

Barré, Virginie
Galerie Loevenbruck

Barriball, Anna
Frith Street Gallery

Barry, Robert
Yvon Lambert Paris/New York

van Bart, Hannah
Marianne Boesky Gallery

Bartana, Yael
Annet Gelink Gallery

Barth, Uta
Alison Jacques Gallery
Andréhn-Schiptjenko
Sies + Höke
Tanya Bonakdar Gallery

Bartolini, Massimo
Frith Street Gallery
Galleria Massimo De Carlo
Magazzino d'Arte Moderna

Bas, Hernan
Daniel Reich Gallery
Frederic Snitzer Gallery
Sandroni Rey
Victoria Miro Gallery

Baselitz, Georg
Galerie Thaddaeus Ropac
Patrick Painter, Inc., Inc.

Bashi, Tatsurou
Blum & Poe

Basquiat, Jean-Michel
Cheim & Read
Kukje Gallery

Baudart, Eric
Galerie Chez Valentin

Baudrexel, Florian
Arndt & Partner Berlin/Zurich

Bauer, John
Bellwether

Bauer, Marc
Galerie Praz-Delavallade

Bauer, Michael
Hotel

Baum, Erica
D'Amelio Terras

Bavington, Tim
Jack Shainman Gallery

Baxter, Bhakti
Frederic Snitzer Gallery
Galerie Emmanuel Perrotin

Bayrle, Thomas
Galerie Barbara Weiss

Bazak, Ivan
Lia Rumma

Beck, Robert
CRG Gallery

Becker, Julie
Greene Naftali

Becker, Matias
Galerie Almine Rech

Becket, Charlotte
Taxter & Spengemann

Beckwith, Patterson
Daniel Hug

Bedford, Whitney
D'Amelio Terras

Beech, John
Peter Blum Gallery

Beecroft, Vanessa
COSMIC Galerie
Galerie Meyer Kainer
Lia Rumma

Beekman, Tjebbe
Galerie Diana Stigter

de Beer, Sue
Arndt & Partner Berlin/Zurich
Marianne Boesky Gallery
Sandroni Rey

Beer Tjorg, Douglas
Mitchell-Innes & Nash
Produzentengalerie Hamburg

Bell, Dirk
The Modern Institute

Bell-Smith, Michael
Foxy Production

Belott, Brian
CANADA

Benassi, Elisabetta
Magazzino d'Arte Moderna

Benat, Laetitia
COSMIC Galerie

Benedict, Matthew
Mai 36 Galerie

Ben-Gal, Avner
Bortolami Dayan

Benglis, Lynda
Cheim & Read

Beninati, Manfredi
James Cohan Gallery

Bennett, Amy
Galleri Magnus Karlsson

Benson, Frank
Taxter & Spengemann

Ben-Tor, Tamy
Zach Feuer Gallery

Berkeley, Tanyth
Bellwether

Berkenblit, Ellen
Anton Kern Gallery

Bernhardt, Katherine
CANADA

Bernstrup, Tobias
COSMIC Galerie

Besemer, Linda
Angles Gallery

Beshty, Walead
China Art Objects
Wallspace

Bessone, Amy
David Kordansky Gallery

Beuys, Joseph
Ronald Feldman Fine Arts, Inc.

Bickerton, Ashley
Lehmann Maupin

Bigert & Bergström
Galerie Barbara Thumm
Milliken

Bijl, Marc
COSMIC Galerie
The Breeder

Bill, Simon
Stuart Shave/Modern Art

Bircken, Alexandra
Herald St
Birkas, Akos
Galerie EIGEN + ART

Bishton, Ginny
Richard Telles Fine Art

Bisky, Norbert
Leo Koenig, Inc., Inc.

Bismuth, Pierre
COSMIC Galerie
Lisson Gallery
Team Gallery

Bitner, Rhona
CRG Gallery

Björnberg, Mette
Galleri Magnus Karlsson

Black Leotard Front
Daniel Reich Gallery

Blake, Nayland
Matthew Marks Gallery

Blanckart, Olivier
Galerie Loevenbruck

Bleckner, Ross
Lehmann Maupin

Blencke, Hanna-Mari
Daniel Hug

Blue Noses, The
in Situ

Blum, Andrea
in Situ

Boberg, Oliver
Angles Gallery

Bock, John
Anton Kern Gallery
Galerie Meyer Kainer
Sommer Contemporary Art
Stella Lohaus Gallery

Boehm, Armin
Johnen/Schöttle
Meyer Riegger Galerie

Boetti, Alighiero
Galleria Massimo De Carlo

Bogacka, Agata
Galerie Meyer Kainer

Boggio Sella, Marco
COSMIC Galerie
John Connelly Presents

Bogin, Greg
Leo Koenig, Inc., Inc.

von Bonin, Cosima
Friedrich Petzel Gallery

Borland, Christine
Lisson Gallery
Sean Kelly Gallery

Bornstein, Jennifer
Blum & Poe
greengrassi

Boroson, Lee
Sara Meltzer Gallery

Borremans, Michaël
David Zwirner
Zeno X Gallery

Bossut, Etienne
Galerie Chez Valentin

Botes, Conrad
Michael Stevenson Gallery

Botha, Wim
Michael Stevenson Gallery

Boudier, Véronique
Galerie Chez Valentin

Bourgeois, Louise
Carolina Nitsch
Cheim & Read
Hauser & Wirth Zürich London
Kukje Gallery
Peter Blum Gallery

Bove, Carol
Georg Kargl
Hotel

Bovo, Marie
Galerie Kamel Mennour

Bowers, Andrea
Galerie Praz-Delavallade
Sara Meltzer Gallery

Bowling, Katherine
Greenberg Van Doren Gallery

Boyce, Martin
Galerie Eva Presenhuber
Johnen/Schöttle
Tanya Bonakdar Gallery
The Modern Institute

Bozhkov, Daniel
Andrew Kreps Gallery

Braden, Tim
Timothy Taylor Gallery

Bradley, Joe
CANADA

Bradley, Slater
Blum & Poe
Taka Ishii Gallery
Team Gallery

Braeckman, Dirk
Zeno X Gallery

Braman, Sarah
CANADA

von Brandenburg, Ulla
Produzentengalerie Hamburg

Brannon, Matthew
David Kordansky Gallery
Friedrich Petzel Gallery
Jan Winkelmannn/Berlin

van Bruggen, Coosje
PaceWildenstein

Braun, Lutz
Galerie Christian Nagel

Braun, Matti
Daniel Hug

Brauntuch, Troy
Friedrich Petzel Gallery
Mai 36 Galerie

Breitz, Candice
galleria francesca kaufmann

Kukje Gallery
Shugoarts
White Cube/Jay Jopling

Bremer, Sebastiaan
Galerie Barbara Thumm

Brenner, Birgit
Galerie EIGEN + ART

Breuning, Olaf
Galerie Meyer Kainer
Kodama
Metro Pictures

Brodahl, Cris
Marc Foxx
The Approach

Brodsky, Alexander
Ronald Feldman Fine Arts, Inc.

van den Broek, Koen
White Cube/Jay Jopling

Broisat, Benoît
COSMIC Galerie

Bronson, AA
John Connelly Presents

Bronson, Jessica
Anna Helwing Gallery

Bronstein, Pablo
Herald St

Brooks, James
Greenberg Van Doren Gallery

Broomé, Thomas
Galleri Magnus Karlsson

Brouwn, Stanley
Yvon Lambert Paris/New York

Brown, Delia
D'Amelio Terras

Brown, Glenn
Patrick Painter, Inc.

Brüning, Bettina
Gavlak

Brus, Günter
Galerie Krinzinger

de Bruyckere, Berlinde
Galleria Continua
Hauser & Wirth Zürich London
Yvon Lambert Paris/New York

Bryce, Fernando
Galerie Barbara Thumm

Buchanan, Roderick
Galerie Praz-Delavallade

Büchel, Christoph
Hauser & Wirth Zürich London

Buckingham, Matthew
Murray Guy

Bucklow, Christopher
Paul Kasmin Gallery Gallery

Budny, Michal
Johnen/Schöttle

Bujnowski, Rafal
Johnen/Schöttle

Bulloch, Angela
Galerie Eva Presenhuber

Bunn, David
Angles Gallery

Burden, Chris
Galerie Krinzinger
Galleria Massimo De Carlo

Buren, Daniel
Bortolami Dayan
Galerie Kamel Mennour
Galleria Continua

Burgert, Jonas
Produzentengalerie Hamburg

Burghard
Jan Winkelmann/Berlin

Burghard, Linda
Fredericks & Freiser

Burnham, Linda
Fredericks & Freiser

Burr, Tom
Galerie Almine Rech
Galleria Franco Noero
Stuart Shave/Modern Art

Burri, Alberto
Lia Rumma

Burton, Jeff
Casey Kaplan
Galleria Franco Noero
Taka Ishii Gallery

Burton, Richmond
Cheim & Read

Bustamante, Jean-Marc
Timothy Taylor Gallery

Butzer, André
Galerie Guido W. Baudach
Patrick Painter, Inc.

Byrne, Nicholas
Vilma Gold

Cabrera, Margarita
Sara Meltzer Gallery

Cabrita Reis, Pedro
Haunch of Venison
Magazzino d'Arte Moderna
Mai 36 Galerie

Cadio, Damien
Galerie Almine Rech

Cahn, Miriam
Zeno X Gallery

Cain, Peter
Galerie Aurel Scheibler
Matthew Marks Gallery

Caivano, Guillermo
IBID Projects

Caivano, Varda
Victoria Miro Gallery

Calame, Ingrid
James Cohan Gallery

Calder, Alexander
Kukje Gallery
PaceWildenstein

Calderwood, Matt
Taxter & Spengemann

Calkins, Case
D'Amelio Terras

Calle, Sophie
Arndt & Partner Berlin/Zurich
Galerie Emmanuel Perrotin

Calvin, Brian
Anton Kern Gallery
Corvi-Mora
Marc Foxx

Campanini, Pierpaolo
Blum & Poe
Corvi-Mora
galleria francesca kaufmann

Campbell, Neil
Galleria Franco Noero

Canaday, Steve
Black Dragon Society

Cantor, Mircea
Magazzino d'Arte Moderna
Yvon Lambert Paris/New York

Cape, Francis
Murray Guy

Caporael, Suzanne
Greenberg Van Doren Gallery

Caravaggio, Gianni
galleria francesca kaufmann

Cardells, Joan
Galeria Pepe Cobo

Cardells, Maggie
galleria francesca kaufmann

Cardiff & Bures Miller, Janet & George
Galerie Barbara Weiss

Cariello, Letizia
Galleria Continua

Caro, Anthony
Mitchell-Innes & Nash

Carpenter, Merlin
Galerie Christian Nagel

Carpinteros, Los
in Situ
Sean Kelly Gallery

Carr, Carolyn
Gavlak

Carron, Valentin
Galerie Eva Presenhuber
Galerie Praz-Delavallade

Carter, Nathan
Casey Kaplan

Carter
Hotel
Jack Hanley Gallery

Casebere, James
Lisson Gallery
Sean Kelly Gallery

Castellani, Enrico
Lia Rumma

Castillo Deball, Mariana
Adamski Gallery for
Contemporary Art

Cattelan, Maurizio
Galerie Emmanuel Perrotin
Galleria Massimo De Carlo

Caughey, Samara
David Kordansky Gallery

Cave, Nick
Jack Shainman Gallery

Cecchini, Loris
Galleria Continua

Celmins, Vija
Carolina Nitsch

Cerletty, Mathew
Rivington Arms

Cesarco, Alejandro
Murray Guy

Ceylan, Taner
Galerist

Cha, Xavier
Taxter & Spengemann

Chalayan, Hussein
Galerist

Chamberlain, John
PaceWildenstein

Chan, Paul
Greene Naftali

Chapman, Jake & Dinos
White Cube/Jay Jopling

Chapman, Jesse
Shane Campbell Gallery

de Chavez, Leslie
Arario Gallery

Chen, Yi
Marianne Boesky Gallery

Chetwynd, Spartacus
Herald St

Chisholm, Ross
IBID Projects

Cho, Duck-Hyun
Kukje Gallery

Chodzko, Adam
Galleria Franco Noero

Chu, Anne
303 Gallery
Victoria Miro Gallery

Chun, Kwang-Young
Kukje Gallery

Chung, Jay
Marc Foxx

Chung, Suejin
Arario Gallery

Chunn, Nancy
Ronald Feldman Fine Arts, Inc.

Churm, Rob
Sorcha Dallas

Cinto, Sandra
Tanya Bonakdar Gallery

Claerbout, David
Hauser & Wirth Zürich London
Johnen/Schöttle
Yvon Lambert Paris/New York

Clark, Kimberly
COSMIC Galerie

Claydon, Steven
David Kordansky Gallery
Hotel

Clayton Brothers
Bellwether

Clegg & Guttman
Galerie Christian Nagel
Georg Kargl
Lia Rumma

Clements, Dawn
Pierogi

Cline, Michael
Daniel Reich Gallery

Close, Chuck
PaceWildenstein
White Cube/Jay Jopling

de Cock, Jan
Sommer Contemporary Art
Stella Lohaus Gallery

Coffin, Peter
Andrew Kreps Gallery
Herald St

Cohen, Lynne
in Situ

Colburn, Martha
Galerie Diana Stigter

Coleman, James
Johnen/Schöttle

Colen, Dan
Peres Projects

Collier, Anne
Corvi-Mora
Jack Hanley Gallery
Marc Foxx

Collins, Andy
Corvi-Mora
Marc Foxx

Collins, Hannah
GERING & LóPEZ GALLERY

Collins, Phil
Kerlin Gallery
Tanya Bonakdar Gallery

Collishaw, Mat
COSMIC Galerie
Stuart Shave/Modern Art
Tanya Bonakdar Gallery

Comte, Serge
Galerie Almine Rech

Conley, Brian
Milliken

Connors, Matt
The Breeder

Conrad, Tony
Greene Naftali

Cooke, Nigel
Blum & Poe
Stuart Shave/Modern Art

Coolidge, Miles
Casey Kaplan

Coombes, Henry
Anna Helwing Gallery
Sorcha Dallas

Cooper, Fredric
Snitzer Gallery

Copeland, Bjorn
China Art Objects

Copley, William N.
David Nolan Gallery

Corbijn, Anton
Zeno X Gallery

Cordova, William
Arndt & Partner Berlin/Zurich

Corillon, Patrick
in Situ

Costello, Devon
Taxter & Spengemann

Cottingham, Keith
Ronald Feldman Fine Arts, Inc.
Annet Gelink Gallery
Galerie Praz-Delavallade

Craft, Liz
Alison Jacques Gallery
Marianne Boesky Gallery
Peres Projects

Cragg, Tony
Galerie Chantal Crousel
Galerie Thaddaeus Ropac
Lisson Gallery

Craig-Martin, Jessica
Greenberg Van Doren Gallery

Craun, Justin
Fredericks & Freiser

Creed, Martin
Hauser & Wirth Zürich London
Johnen/Schöttle
Marc Foxx

Crewdson, Gregory
White Cube/Jay Jopling

de Crignis, Rudolf
Peter Blum Gallery

Croitoru, Alexandra
Plan B

Cross, Dorothy
Frith Street Gallery
Kerlin Gallery

Crotty, Russell
CRG Gallery

Crow, Rosson
CANADA

Croxson, Joel
Dicksmith Gallery

Crumb, R.
David Zwirner

de la Cruz, Angela
Galerie Krinzinger
Lisson Gallery

Cuoghi, Roberto
Galleria Massimo De Carlo

Curiel, Christian
Lehmann Maupin

Curry, Aaron
David Kordansky Gallery

Cvijanovic, Adam
Bellwether

da Cunha, Alexandre
Vilma Gold

Dack, Sean
Daniel Reich Gallery
David Kordansky Gallery

Dafflon, Stéphane
Jan Winkelmann/Berlin

Dahlem, Björn
Galerie Guido W. Baudach
Hiromi Yoshii

Dahn, Walter
Yvon Lambert Paris/New York

Damasceno, José
The Project
Thomas Dane Gallery

Dammann, Martin
Galerie Barbara Thumm
Georg Kargl

Daniels, William
Marc Foxx
Vilma Gold

Danke, Tobias and Raphael
Adamski Gallery for
Contemporary Art

Darboven, Hanne
Galerie Crone

David, Franck
Galerie Chez Valentin

Davis, Gerald
Black Dragon Society
John Connelly Presents

Davis, Kate
Sorcha Dallas

Davis, Tim
Greenberg Van Doren Gallery

Dawson, Verne
Galerie Eva Presenhuber
Victoria Miro Gallery

Day, E.V.
Carolina Nitsch
Deitch Projects

Deacon, Richard
Galerie Thomas Schulte
Lisson Gallery

Dean, Tacita
Frith Street Gallery

Declercq, Alain
Galerie Loevenbruck

Decrauzat, Philippe
Galerie Praz-Delavallade

Dejanoff, Plamen
Galerie Meyer Kainer
Jan Winkelmann/Berlin

Deller, Jeremy
The Modern Institute

Dellsperger, Brice
Team Gallery

Delvoye, Wim
Galerie Emmanuel Perrotin

Demand, Thomas
303 Gallery
Taka Ishii Gallery
Victoria Miro Gallery

Demmerle, Yannick
Arndt & Partner Berlin/Zurich

Derges, Susan
Paul Kasmin Gallery Gallery

Deroubaix, Damien
in Situ

Dewan, Brian
Pierogi

Devriendt, Robert
Galerie Loevenbruck

Dewar & Gregory Gicquel, Daniel
Galerie Loevenbruck

Di Genova, Nicholas
Fredericks & Freiser

DiBenedetto, Steve
David Nolan Gallery

Dicke, Amie
Galerie Diana Stigter
Peres Projects

Dickinson, Jeremy
Angles Gallery
Sara Meltzer Gallery

diCorcia, Philip-Lorca
Galerie Almine Rech

Diebenkorn, Richard
Greenberg Van Doren Gallery

Diederix, Elspeth
Galerie Diana Stigter

Diefenbach, Andreas
Galerie Christian Nagel

Dine, Jim
PaceWildenstein

Dion, Mark
Galerie Christian Nagel
Georg Kargl
in Situ
Tanya Bonakdar Gallery

Djurberg, Nathalie
Zach Feuer Gallery

Doberauer, Anke
Mai 36 Galerie

Dodge, Jason
Casey Kaplan
Taka Ishii Gallery
Yvon Lambert Paris/New York

Dodge, Tomory
Alison Jacques Gallery
CRG Gallery

Dodiya, Anju
Nature Morte

Dodiya, Atul
Nature Morte

Doherty, Willie
Galeria Pepe Cobo
Kerlin Gallery

Doig, Peter
Victoria Miro Gallery

Dole Recio, Lecia
Adamski Gallery for
Contemporary Art
Richard Telles Fine Art

Doll, Tatjana
Galerie Gebr. Lehmann

Dollinger, Olivier
Galerie Chez Valentin

de Dominicis, Gino
Lia Rumma

Donachie, Kaye
John Connelly Presents
Maureen Paley
Peres Projects

Donnelly, Trisha
Casey Kaplan
Galerie Eva Presenhuber

Donovan, Tara
PaceWildenstein

Dopitová, Milena
Ronald Feldman Fine Arts, Inc.

Dorner, Helmut
Sean Kelly Gallery

Dost, Stephanie
Marianne Boesky Gallery

Douglas, Stan
David, Zwirner
Zeno X Gallery

Dowd, Luke
Hotel

Dragicevic, Milena
IBID Projects

Drain, Jim
Greene Naftali

Draper, Markus
Galerie Gebr. Lehmann

Drescher, Jürgen
Mai 36

Driesen, Stef
Alison Jacques Gallery
Harris Lieberman
Marc Foxx

Drummond, Blaise
Galerie Loevenbruck

Dube, Anita
Galerie Almine Rech
Nature Morte

Dubossarsky and Vinogradov
Galerie Krinzinger
Vilma Gold

Dubuffet, Jean
PaceWildenstein

Dumas, Marlene
Frith Street Gallery
Zeno X Gallery

Dunham, Carroll
David Nolan Gallery
White Cube/Jay Jopling

Dupont, Richard
Carolina Nitsch

Durant, Sam
Blum & Poe
Galerie Praz-Delavallade

Duyckaerts, Eric
Galerie Emmanuel Perrotin

Dyrenforth, Jacob
Wallspace

Dzama, Marcel
David Zwirner
Galleri Magnus Karlsson
Sies + Höke
Timothy Taylor Gallery

Eastman, Mari
Sies + Höke

Ebner, Shannon
Wallspace

Eder, Martin
Galerie EIGEN + ART
Marianne Boesky Gallery

Edmier, Keith
Friedrich Petzel Gallery

Edwards, Benjamin
Greenberg Van Doren Gallery

Eggerer, Thomas
Richard Telles Fine Art

Eggleston, William
Carolina Nitsch
Cheim & Read
Victoria Miro Gallery

Eichhorn, Maria
Galerie Barbara Weiss
Galerie Eva Presenhuber

Eide Einarsson, Gardar
Team Gallery

Eisenman, Nicole
Galerie Barbara Weiss
Leo Koenig, Inc.

Eitel, Tim
Galerie EIGEN + ART

Eliasson, Olafur
Carolina Nitsch
Tanya Bonakdar Gallery

Elizabeth, Taylor Alison
James Cohan Gallery

Ellen Mark, Mary
Marianne Boesky Gallery

Ellis, Sharon
Greenberg Van Doren Gallery

Elmgreen & Ingar Dragset, Michael
Galerie Emmanuel Perrotin
Galleria Massimo De Carlo
Taka Ishii Gallery
Tanya Bonakdar Gallery

Elrod, Jeff
Fredericks & Freiser

van der Elsken, Ed
Annet Gelink Gallery

Elsner, Slawomir
Galerie Gebr. Lehmann
Johnen/Schöttle
Sutton Lane

Emin, Tracey
Lehmann Maupin
White Cube/Jay Jopling

Eneblom, Niklas
Galleri Magnus Karlsson

Enli, Zhang
Hauser & Wirth Zürich London
Hiromi Yoshii

Enoksson, Per
Milliken

Enomoto, Koichi
Hiromi Yoshii

Enright, Brock
Vilma Gold

Erkmen, Ayse
Galerie Barbara Weiss
Galerist

Erlich, Léandro
Galerie Emmanuel Perrotin

Esber, James
Pierogi

Espaliú, Pepe
Galeria Pepe Cobo

Espinosa, John
Frederic Snitzer Gallery
Sandroni Rey

do Espírito Santo, Iran
Sean Kelly Gallery

Essenhigh, Inka
303 Gallery
Victoria Miro Gallery

Esser, Elger
Galerie Thaddaeus Ropac
Johnen/Schöttle

Esteve, Lionel
Galerie Emmanuel Perrotin

Estlund, Phillip
Gavlak

Ethridge, Roe
Andrew Kreps Gallery
greengrassi
Mai 36 Galerie

Evans, Chris
Store

Evans, Dick
Maureen Paley

Evans, Simon
Jack Hanley Gallery

Export, Valie
Patrick Painter, Inc.

Exposito, Bart
Black Dragon Society

Ezawa, Kota
Murray Guy

Fabien
Galerie Kamel Mennour

Fabre, Jan
Magazzino d'Arte Moderna

Fabrizio, Leo
Galerie Kamel Mennour

Fagundo, Pete
Shane Campbell Gallery

Fahlstrom, Brian
Marc Foxx

Fahlström, Öyvind
Galerie Aurel Scheibler

Fairhurst, Angus
Georg Kargl
Paul Kasmin Gallery

Faldbakken, Matias
Galerie Diana Stigter

Fänge, Jens
Galleri Magnus Karlsson

Farocki, Harun
Greene Naftali

Faunce, Justin
Leo Koenig, Inc.

Faust, Gretchen
greengrassi

Faust, Jeanne
Meyer Riegger Galerie

Favaretto, Lara
Galleria Franco Noero

Fecteau, Vincent
Marc Foxx

Federle, Helmut
Peter Blum Gallery

Feher, Tony
D'Amelio Terras

Feinstein, Rachel
Corvi-Mora
Marianne Boesky Gallery

Feintuch, Robert
CRG Gallery

Feldmann, Friederike
Galerie Barbara Weiss

Feldmann, Hans-Peter
303 Gallery
Johnen/Schöttle

Fernandez, Diego
Galerie Christian Nagel

Fernández, Teresita
Lehmann Maupin

Ferris, Dee
Corvi-Mora

Finch, Spencer
Lisson Gallery
Yvon Lambert Paris/New York

Fine, Jane
Pierogi

Finneran, John
Rivington Arms

Fischer, Urs
Galerie Eva Presenhuber
The Modern Institute

Fischer / Maroan el Sani, Nina
Galerie EIGEN + ART

Fischli & Weiss, Peter & David
Galerie Eva Presenhuber
Matthew Marks Gallery

Fisher, Kim
China Art Objects
John Connelly Presents
Shane Campbell Gallery
The Modern Institute

Fisher, Morgan
Adamski Gallery for
    Contemporary Art
China Art Objects

Fisher, Naomi
Frederic Snitzer Gallery
Galerie Emmanuel Perrotin

Fisher, Urs
Galleria Massimo De Carlo

Fishman, Louise
Cheim & Read

Fisk, Lars
Taxter & Spengemann

Fiskin, Judy
Angles Gallery

Fitzpatrick, Tony
Pierogi

Flamm, Christian
Alison Jacques Gallery

Flanagan, Barry
Paul Kasmin Gallery

Flannigan, Moyna
Sara Meltzer Gallery

Flechtner, Harrell
in Situ
Jack Hanley Gallery

Flechtner, Thomas
Marianne Boesky Gallery

Fletcher, Saul
Anton Kern Gallery

Fleury, Sylvie
Galerie Eva Presenhuber
Galerie Thaddaeus Ropac

Flexner, Roland
Galleria Massimo De Carlo

Flores, Mark
Alison Jacques Gallery
David Kordansky Gallery

Floyer, Ceal
303 Gallery
Lisson Gallery

Fock, Carsten
Jan Winkelmann/Berlin

Fonesca, Caio
Paul Kasmin Gallery

Ford, Walter
Paul Kasmin Gallery

Fowler, Luke
The Modern Institute

Fowler, Will
David Kordansky Gallery

Fox, Terry
Ronald Feldman Fine Arts, Inc.

Framis, Alicia
Annet Gelink Gallery

Francis, Mark
Galerie Thomas Schulte
Kerlin Gallery

François, Michel
Bortolami Dayan

Frank, Natalie
Mitchell-Innes & Nash

Fraser, Andrea
Friedrich Petzel Gallery
Galerie Christian Nagel

Fraser, Pamela
Casey Kaplan

Frecon, Suzan
Peter Blum Gallery

Frédéric, Schnyder Jean
Galerie Barbara Weiss

Freeman, Jonah
Andrew Kreps Gallery

Freeman/Phelan
John Connelly Presents

Frerichs, Marten
Galerie Jan Wentrup

Freud, Lucian
Matthew Marks Gallery
Timothy Taylor Gallery

Friedl, Peter
Sara Meltzer Gallery

Fries, Pia
CRG Gallery
Mai 36 Galerie

Fritsch, Katharina
Matthew Marks Gallery
White Cube/Jay Jopling

Frize, Bernard
Galerie Emmanuel Perrotin
Patrick Painter, Inc.

Froment, Aurélien
COSMIC Galerie
Store

Frost, Alex
Sorcha Dallas
Peter Blum Gallery

Fudge, Carl
Ronald Feldman Fine Arts, Inc.

Fujimoto, Yukio
Shugoarts

Fulton, Hamish
Maureen Paley

Funk, Karel
303 Gallery

Furnas, Barnaby
Marianne Boesky Gallery
Stuart Shave/Modern Art

Furunishi, Noriko
Murray Guy

Fusco, Coco
The Project

Fuss, Adam
Cheim & Read
Timothy Taylor Gallery

Gabbiani, Francesca
Patrick Painter, Inc.

Gabellone, Giuseppe
Galerie Emmanuel Perrotin
greengrassi

Gaines, Charles
Adamski Gallery for
    Contemporary Art

Gallaccio, Anya
Annet Gelink Gallery
Blum & Poe
Lehmann Maupin
Thomas Dane Gallery

Gallace, Maureen
303 Gallery
Kerlin Gallery
Maureen Paley

Gallagher, Ellen
Hauser & Wirth Zürich London

Galloway, Munro
Murray Guy

Gander, Ryan
Annet Gelink Gallery
Marc Foxx
Store

Garaicoa, Carlos
Galleria Continua

Garcia-Alix, Alberto
Galerie Kamel Mennour

Gardner, Tim
303 Gallery
Stuart Shave/Modern Art

Garrett, Christopher
Jack Hanley Gallery

Gartrell, Amy
Daniel Reich Gallery

Garutti, Alberto
Magazzino d'Arte Moderna

Gaskell, Anna
Yvon Lambert Paris/New York

Gatson, Rico
Ronald Feldman Fine Arts, Inc.

Gavaisse, Vasso
The Breeder

Gediz, Leyla
Galerist

Geers, Kendell
Galleria Continua
Yvon Lambert Paris/New York

Geis, Axel
Galerie Jan Wentrup

Gelitin
Galerie Emmanuel Perrotin

Galerie Meyer Kainer
Galleria Massimo De Carlo

Gennari, Francesco
Johnen/Schöttle

Genzken, Isa
David Zwirner
Hauser & Wirth Zürich London

Gerber, Gaylen
Daniel Hug

Gersht, Ori
Angles Gallery
CRG Gallery

Ghazi, Babak
Galerie Chez Valentin

Ghenie, Adrian
Plan B

Gianakos, Steve
Fredericks & Freiser

Gibbs, Ewan
Timothy Taylor Gallery

Giehler, Torben
Arndt & Partner Berlin/Zurich
Leo Koenig, Inc.

Gilbert & George
Galerie Thaddaeus Ropac
Lehmann Maupin
White Cube/Jay Jopling

Gillick, Liam
Casey Kaplan
Corvi-Mora
Galerie Eva Presenhuber
Galerie Meyer Kainer

Gilmore, Kate
Pierogi

Ginckels, Pieterjan
Sommer Contemporary Art
Stella Lohaus Gallery

Giordano, Jacin
Frederic Snitzer Gallery

Giorno, John
Galerie Almine Rech

Gispert, Luis
Frederic Snitzer Gallery
Zach Feuer Gallery

Gitman, Victoria
David Nolan Gallery

Glasser, Jason
Galerie Kamel Mennour

Globus, Amy
D'Amelio Terras

Gmelin, Felix
Milliken

Gober, Robert
Matthew Marks Gallery

Godbold, David
Jack Hanley Gallery
Kerlin Gallery

Goicolea, Anthony
Galerie Aurel Scheibler
Sandroni Rey

Goldberg, Neil
Sara Meltzer Gallery

Goldblatt, David
Michael Stevenson Gallery

Goldin, Nan
Matthew Marks Gallery
Yvon Lambert Paris/New York

Goldstein, Jack
Mitchell-Innes & Nash

Golia, Piero
Bortolami Dayan
COSMIC Galerie

Golub, Leon
Ronald Feldman Fine Arts, Inc.

González, Maria Elena
The Project

Gonzalez & Russom,
Delia & Gavin R.
Daniel Reich Gallery

Gordon, Daniel
Zach Feuer Gallery

Gordon, Douglas
Carolina Nitsch
Yvon Lambert Paris/New York

Gordon, Janine
Galerie Kamel Mennour

Gormley, Antony
Galerie Thaddaeus Ropac
Sean Kelly Gallery
White Cube/Jay Jopling

Gottlieb, Adolph
PaceWildenstein

Goudzwaard, Kees
Zeno X Gallery

Gowda, Sheela
Nature Morte

Grabner, Michelle
Shane Campbell Gallery

Graf, Manuel
Johann König

Graf, Yesim Akdeniz
Galerist

Graham, Dan
Galerie Meyer Kainer
Hauser & Wirth Zürich London
Johnen/Schöttle
Lisson Gallery

Graham, Paul
Greenberg Van Doren Gallery

Graham, Rodney
303 Gallery
Hauser & Wirth Zürich London
Johnen/Schöttle
Lisson Gallery

Granhert, Henriette
Sutton Lane

Grannan, Katy
Greenberg Van Doren Gallery

Granser, Peter
Galerie Kamel Mennour

Granular Synthesis
Lia Rumma

Grassie, Andrew
Maureen Paley

Grasso, Laurent
Galerie Chez Valentin

Grauer, Phil
CANADA

Greely, Hannah
Black Dragon Society

Green, Brent
Bellwether

Green, Renée
Galerie Christian Nagel

Green, Taft
Richard Telles Fine Art

Greenbaum, Joanne
D'Amelio Terras
Shane Campbell Gallery

Greene, Matt
Peres Projects

Greene, Robert
Robert Miller Gallery

Greenfort, Tue
Johann König

Grenet, Yves
Galerie Chez Valentin

Griffiths, Brian
Vilma Gold

Grimonprez, Johan
Sean Kelly Gallery

Gronemeyer, Ellen
greengrassi

Grönlund/Nisunen,
Tommi & Petteri
Andréhn-Schiptjenko

Grotjahn, Mark
Anton Kern Gallery
Blum & Poe
Shane Campbell Gallery

Gu, Wenda
Galerie Almine Rech

Guangyi, Wang
Arario Gallery

Gundersdorf, Carrie
Shane Campbell Gallery

Gunning, Lucy
Greene Naftali

Gupta, Shilpa
Nature Morte

Gupta, Subodh
in Situ
Jack Shainman Gallery
Nature Morte

Gursky, Andreas
Lia Rumma
Matthew Marks Gallery
White Cube/Jay Jopling

Guston, Philip
Timothy Taylor Gallery

Joshua Cooper, Thomas
Haunch of Venison

Ju Lim, Won
Patrick Painter, Inc.

Judd, Donald
Carolina Nitsch
Lia Rumma
PaceWildenstein

Jakub Ziolkowski, Julian
Hauser & Wirth Zürich London

Julien, Isaac
Metro Pictures
Victoria Miro Gallery
Yvon Lambert Paris/New York

Jung, Yeondoo
Kukje Gallery

Jungen, Brian
Casey Kaplan

Jurczak, Dorota
Corvi-Mora

Kabakov, Ilya
Galleria Continua
Lia Rumma

Kabakov, Ilya & Emilia
Sean Kelly Gallery

Kagami, Ken
Galerie Krinzinger

Kahlhamer, Brad
Andréhn-Schiptjenko
Deitch Projects
Stuart Shave/Modern Art

Kahrs, Johannes
Galerie Almine Rech
Zeno X Gallery

Kaino, Glenn
The Project

Kakitani, Tomoki
Kodama

Kaleka, Ranbir
Nature Morte

Kalenderian, Raffi
Black Dragon Society

Kalki, Michael
Galerie Jan Wentrup

Kallat, Jitish
Arario Gallery
Nature Morte

Kallioinen, Matti
Milliken

Kalmbach Michael
Robert Miller Gallery

Kaneuji, Teppei
Kodama

Kang, Hyung-Goo
Arario Gallery

Kaplan, Peggy Jarrell
Ronald Feldman Fine Arts, Inc.

Kapoor, Anish
Galleria Continua
Kukje Gallery
Lisson Gallery

Kaprow, Allan
Hauser & Wirth Zürich London

Karlsson, Johanna
Galleri Magnus Karlsson

Karubian, Charles
Black Dragon Society

Kass, Deborah
Paul Kasmin Gallery

Katchadourian, Nina
Sara Meltzer Gallery

Kato, Mika
White Cube/Jay Jopling

Katz, Alex
Galerie Barbara Thumm
Galerie Thaddaeus Ropac
PaceWildenstein
Peter Blum Gallery
Timothy Taylor Gallery

Kauffman, Craig
GERING & LóPEZ GALLERY

Kauper, Kurt
Deitch Projects

Kavallieratos, Dionisis
The Breeder

Kawahara, Naoto
Taka Ishii Gallery

Kawara, On
David Zwirner
Hauser & Wirth Zürich London
Yvon Lambert Paris/New York

Kawauchi, Rinko
Galeria Pepe Cobo

Kay, Edward
Dicksmith Gallery

Keegan, Matt
D'Amelio Terras

Keïta, Seydou (The Estate of)
Sean Kelly Gallery

Kelley, Mike
Metro Pictures
Patrick Painter, Inc.

Kelly, Ellsworth
Matthew Marks Gallery

Kelm, Annette
Johann König
Marc Foxx

Kendrick, Mel
David Nolan Gallery

Kentridge, William
Lia Rumma

van Kerckhoven, Anne-Mie
Galerie Barbara Thumm
Zeno X Gallery

Kern, Richard
Hotel

Kerr, Andrew
The Modern Institute

de Keyser, Raoul
David Zwirner
Galerie Barbara Weiss
Zeno X Gallery

Khalid, Aisha
Corvi-Mora

Khan, Hassan
Galerie Chantal Crousel

Khan, Idris
Galerie Thomas Schulte
Victoria Miro Gallery
Yvon Lambert Paris/New York

Khedoori, Rachel
David Zwirner
Hauser & Wirth Zürich London

Khedoori, Toba
David Zwirner

Kher, Barti
Jack Shainman Gallery
Nature Morte
Arario Gallery

Kiaer, Ian
Alison Jacques Gallery
Tanya Bonakdar Gallery

Kiefer, Anselm
Galerie Thaddaeus Ropac
Lia Rumma
White Cube/Jay Jopling
Yvon Lambert Paris/New York

Kielar, Anya
Daniel Reich Gallery

Kienholz, Ed & Nancy
Haunch of Venison

Kilimnik, Karen
303 Gallery
Galerie Eva Presenhuber

Kim, Hanna
Arario Gallery

Kim, Inbae
Arario Gallery

Kim, Soo
Sandroni Rey

Kimsooja
Peter Blum Gallery
The Project

Kimura, Yuki
Kodama
Taka Ishii Gallery

King, Scott
Bortolami Dayan
Herald St

Kippenberger, Martin
Metro Pictures

Kirkpatrick, Julie
Black Dragon Society

Kleberg, Anna
Andréhn-Schiptjenko

Kleckner, John
Peres Projects

Klein, Carla
Annet Gelink Gallery
Tanya Bonakdar Gallery

Kles, Henning
Arndt & Partner Berlin/Zurich
Sandroni Rey

Kluge, Gustav
Produzentengalerie Hamburg

Kneihsl, Erwin
Galerie Guido W. Baudach

Knight, Ross
Team Gallery

Knobloch, Thoralf
Galerie Gebr. Lehmann

Kobayashi, Masato
Shugoarts

Kobe, Martin
White Cube/Jay Jopling

Koelewijn, Job
Sommer Contemporary Art
Stella Lohaus Gallery

Koester, Joachim
Greene Naftali

Koganezawa, Takehito
Hiromi Yoshii

Koh, Terence
Peres Projects

Koizumi, Meiro
Dicksmith Gallery

Kolding, Jakob
Team Gallery

Kolehmainen, Ola
Robert Miller Gallery

Kolk, Douglas
Arndt & Partner Berlin/Zurich

KolKoz
Galerie Emmanuel Perrotin

Komad, Zenita
Galerie Krinzinger

Komar & Melamid
Ronald Feldman Fine Arts, Inc.

Könitz, Alice
Shane Campbell Gallery

Konrad, Karsten
Arndt & Partner Berlin/Zurich

Koo, Bohnchang
Kukje Gallery

Koo, Donghee
Arario Gallery

de Kooning, Willem
Matthew Marks Gallery

Kopystiansky, Igor & Svetlana
Lisson Gallery

Körmeling, John
Zeno X Gallery

Kørner, John
Victoria Miro Gallery

Korpys/Löffler
Meyer Riegger Galerie

Korty, David
China Art Objects
Greene Naftali

Koshlyakov, Valery
Galerie Krinzinger

Kossoff, Leon
Mitchell-Innes & Nash

Kosuth, Joseph
Galerie Almine Rech
Lia Rumma
Sean Kelly Gallery

Koumoundouros, Olga
Adamski Gallery for
Contemporary Art

Kounellis, Jannis
Cheim & Read

Kowski, Uwe
Galerie EIGEN + ART

Krämer, Armin
Corvi-Mora

Krans, Kim
D'Amelio Terras

Krasinski, Edward
Anton Kern Gallery

Krasner, Lee
Robert Miller Gallery

Krawen, Hendik
Lia Rumma

Krebber, Michael
Galerie Chantal Crousel
Galerie Meyer Kainer
Greene Naftali
Maureen Paley
Richard Telles Fine Art

Krinzinger, Angelika
Galerie Krinzinger

Krisanamis, Udomsak
Victoria Miro Gallery

Kristalova, Klara
Galleri Magnus Karlsson

Kroner, Sven
Lia Rumma
Robert Miller Gallery

Kruger, Barbara
Yvon Lambert Paris/New York

Kruip, Germaine
The Approach

Krystufek, Elke
Galerie Barbara Thumm
Georg Kargl

Kudo, Makiko
Marc Foxx

Kuitca, Guillermo
Hauser & Wirth Zürich London

Kumar, Bari
Nature Morte

Kunath, Friedrich
Blum & Poe

Kunin, Julia
Greenberg Van Doren Gallery

Kuri, Gabriel
Galleria Franco Noero

Kurland, Justine
Mitchell-Innes & Nash

Kürten, Stefan
Thomas Dane Gallery

Kusama, Yayoi
Arndt & Partner Berlin/Zurich
Robert Miller Gallery

Kusmirowski, Robert
Johnen/Schöttle

Kusnir, Carlos
Galerie Chez Valentin

Kwartler, Alex
John Connelly Presents

Kwok, Cary
Herald St

L.N., Tallur
Arario Gallery

Labaume, Vincent
Galerie Loevenbruck

Labelle-Rojoux, Arnaud
Galerie Loevenbruck

LaBruce, Bruce
Peres Projects

Ukeles, Mierle Laderman
Ronald Feldman Fine Arts, Inc.

LaDuke, Tom
Angles Gallery

Lai, Phillip
Stuart Shave/Modern Art

Lalanne, Claude and Francois-Xavier
Paul Kasmin Gallery

Lambert, Alix
GERING & LóPEZ GALLERY

Lambie, Jim
Anton Kern Gallery
Galleria Franco Noero
Jack Hanley Gallery
The Modern Institute

Lambri, Luisa
Marc Foxx

Lamers, Kiki
Annet Gelink Gallery

Lamsfuss, Ulrich
Daniel Hug

van Lamsweerde, Inez
Matthew Marks Gallery

Landers, Sean
China Art Objects
Taka Ishii Gallery

Landy, Michael
Thomas Dane Gallery

Langer, Eli
Daniel Hug

van Lankveld, Rezi
Galerie Diana Stigter
The Approach

Lansing-Dreiden
Rivington Arms

Lapinski, Lisa
Johann König
Richard Telles Fine Art

Larsson, Annika
Andréhn-Schiptjenko
COSMIC Galerie

Lasker, Jonathan
Cheim & Read
Galerie Thomas Schulte
Timothy Taylor Gallery

Lassnig, Maria
Hauser & Wirth Zürich London

Latham, John
Lisson Gallery

Lattu, Brandon
Leo Koenig, Inc.

Laurette, Matthieu
Yvon Lambert Paris/New York

LaVerdiere, Julian
Lehmann Maupin

Lavier, Bertrand
Yvon Lambert Paris/New York

Lawler, Louise
Metro Pictures
Yvon Lambert Paris/New York

Lazzarini, Robert
Deitch Projects

Lê, An-My
Murray Guy

Le Va, Barry
David Nolan Gallery

Lea Hucht, Anna
Meyer Riegger Galerie

Leccia, Ange
Galerie Almine Rech

Lee, Dongwook
Arario Gallery

Lee, Hyungkoo
Arario Gallery

Lee, Ji-hyun
Arario Gallery

Lee, Jinyong
Arario Gallery

Lee, Kwangho
Kukje Gallery

Lee, Miyeon
Gavlak

Lee, Seungae
Arario Gallery

Lee, Tim
Lisson Gallery

Lee, Yongbaek
Arario Gallery

Leek, Saskia
Jack Hanley Gallery

Lefcourt, Daniel
Taxter & Spengemann

Leibowitz, Cary
Andrew Kreps Gallery

Lenhardt, Scott
Taxter & Spengemann

Leonard, Zoe
Galeria Pepe Cobo
Yvon Lambert Paris/New York

Lesueur, Natacha
Galerie Praz-Delavallade

Levé, Edouard
Galerie Loevenbruck

Lévêque, Claude
Yvon Lambert Paris/New York

LeWitt, Sol
Lisson Gallery
PaceWildenstein
Yvon Lambert Paris/New York

Liberman, Alexander
Mitchell-Innes & Nash

Lichtenstein, Roy
Mitchell-Innes & Nash

Liddell, Siobhan
CRG Gallery

Liden, Hanna
Rivington Arms

Lieberman, Justin
Sutton Lane
Zach Feuer Gallery

van Lieshout, Atelier
Galerie Krinzinger
Magazzino d'Arte Moderna
Tanya Bonakdar Gallery

Ligon, Glenn
Thomas Dane Gallery
Yvon Lambert Paris/New York

Lijun, Fang
Arario Gallery

Limone, Guy
Galerie Emmanuel Perrotin

Lindena, Kalin
Galerie Christian Nagel
Meyer Riegger Galerie

Lindholm, Petra
Galleri Magnus Karlsson

Ling, Anna
Milliken

Linke, Armin
Magazzino d'Arte Moderna

Linzy, Kalup
Taxter & Spengemann

Lipomi, Chris
Daniel Hug

Lislegaard, Ann
Murray Guy

Little, Graham
Alison Jacques Gallery

Locher, Thomas
Georg Kargl

Lockhart, Sharon
Blum & Poe

Loesch, Dennis
Jan Winkelmann/Berlin

Löffelhardt, Stefan
Galerie Aurel Scheibler

Löfström, Katarina
Jan Winkelmann/Berlin

Loftus, Ed
Jack Hanley Gallery

Lokiec, Tim
Zach Feuer Gallery

Lombardi, Mark
Pierogi

Long, Charles
Tanya Bonakdar Gallery

Long, Richard
Haunch of Venison
James Cohan Gallery

Longo, Robert
Metro Pictures

Lord, Andrew
Galerie Eva Presenhuber

Lou, Liza
White Cube/Jay Jopling

Louis, Morris
Paul Kasmin Gallery

Løw, Camilla
Jack Hanley Gallery
Sutton Lane

Lowe, Nick
Black Dragon Society
John Connelly Presents

Lozano, Lee (The Estate of)
Hauser & Wirth Zürich London

Lozek, Jörg
Sandroni Rey

Lucander
Robert Milliken

Ludlow, Lily
CANADA

Ludwig, Sebastian
Patrick Painter, Inc.

Lukasiewicz, Marcin
Johnen/Schöttle

Lundin, Ulf
Galleri Magnus Karlsson

Lundsager, Eva
Greenberg Van Doren Gallery

Lurie, John
Robert Miller Gallery

Lutz/Guggisberg
Anna Helwing Gallery

M. Den Uyl, Tessa
Lia Rumma

M/M
Haunch of Venison

Ma Yturralde, José
GERING & LóPEZ GALLERY

Macchi, Jorge
Galleria Continua

MacDonald, Euan
Jack Hanley Gallery

Maciejowski, Marcin
Galerie Meyer Kainer
Leo Koenig, Inc.

Mackie, Christina
Herald St

MacKinven, Alastair
Hotel

Macpherson, Sophie
Sorcha Dallas

Madikida, Churchill
Michael Stevenson Gallery

Maeda, Keisuke
Hiromi Yoshii

de Maesschalck, Jan
Zeno X Gallery

Maetake, Yasue
Harris Lieberman

Magill, Elizabeth
Greenberg Van Doren Gallery
Kerlin Gallery
Paragon Press

Mahalchick, Michael
CANADA

Maher, Alice
David Nolan Gallery

Maier, Ati
Pierogi

Maier-Aichen, Florian
303 Gallery
Blum & Poe

Malani, Nalini
Nature Morte

Maljkovic, David
Annet Gelink Gallery

Maloney, Martin
Timothy Taylor Gallery

Maluka, Mustafa
Michael Stevenson Gallery

Man, Victor
Annet Gelink Gallery
Johnen/Schöttle
Plan B
Timothy Taylor Gallery

Man uška, Ján
Meyer Riegger Galerie
Andrew Kreps Gallery

Manders, Mark
Tanya Bonakdar Gallery
Zeno X Gallery

Manetas, Miltos
COSMIC Galerie
Yvon Lambert Paris/New York

Mangano, Domenico
Magazzino d'Arte Moderna

Mangold, Robert
Lisson Gallery
PaceWildenstein

Mania, Andrew
Jack Hanley Gallery
John Connelly Presents
Vilma Gold

Mannig, Martin
Galerie Gebr. Lehmann

Manzelli, Margherita
greengrassi

Mapplethorpe, Robert
Alison Jacques Gallery
Galerie Thaddaeus Ropac
Galerie Thomas Schulte
Mai 36 Galerie
Sean Kelly Gallery

Marcaccio, Fabian
Galerie Thomas Schulte

Marclay, Christian
White Cube/Jay Jopling
Yvon Lambert Paris/New York

Marden, Brice
Matthew Marks Gallery

Marder, Malerie
Maureen Paley

Mardner, Malerie
Greenberg Van Doren Gallery

Marepe
Anton Kern Gallery

Margolis, Alisa
Galerie Diana Stigter
Vilma Gold

Marguerite Teplin, Alexis
Gavlak
Hotel

Maria Barmen, Bianca
Galleri Magnus Karlsson

Maria Sicilia, José
Galerie Chantal Crousel

Marioni, Joseph
Peter Blum Gallery

Marisaldi, Eva
Corvi-Mora

Marker, Chris
Peter Blum Gallery

Markl, Hugo
Galerie Eva Presenhuber

Markowitsch, Rémy
Galerie EIGEN + ART

Marquiss, Duncan
Dicksmith Gallery

Marshall, Maria
COSMIC Galerie
Team Gallery

Martin, Agnes
PaceWildenstein

Martin, Cameron
Greenberg Van Doren Gallery

Martin, Daria
Maureen Paley

Martin, Frankie
CANADA

Martin, Jason
Galerie Thaddaeus Ropac
Lisson Gallery

Martin, Kris
Johann König
Sies + Höke

Martinez, Celaya Enrique
Sara Meltzer Gallery

Maruyama, Naofumi
Shugoarts

Masnyj, Yuri
Metro Pictures
Sutton Lane

Mason, T. Kelly
Daniel Hug

Matelli, Tony
Andrëhn-Schiptjenko
Leo Koenig, Inc.

Matsubara, Soshiro
Hiromi Yoshii

**Matta-Clark, Gordon
(The Estate of)**
Galerie Thomas Schulte
David Zwirner

May Post, Liza
Annet Gelink Gallery

Mayaux, Philippe
Galerie Loevenbruck

Mayer, Hans-Jörg
Galerie Christian Nagel

Mayer, Maix
Galerie EIGEN + ART

Maynard, Gerard
John Connelly Presents

Mc Grath, Tom
Lia Rumma

McBride, Rita
Mai 36 Galerie

McCall, Anthony
Sean Kelly Gallery

McCarren/Fine
Ronald Feldman Fine Arts, Inc.

McCarthy, Alicia
Jack Hanley Gallery

McCarthy, Dan
Anton Kern Gallery
Galerie Gebr. Lehmann

McCarthy, Paul
Hauser & Wirth Zürich London

McCarthy, Sean
Fredericks & Freiser

McCaslin, Matthew
GERING & LóPEZ GALLERY

McClelland, Suzanne
Shane Campbell Gallery

McCollum, Allan
Friedrich Petzel Gallery
Galerie Thomas Schulte

McCracken, John
David Zwirner
Galerie Almine Rech
Hauser & Wirth Zürich London

McDermott & McGough
Cheim & Read

Mcelheny, Josiah
White Cube/Jay Jopling

McEwen, Adam
Jack Hanley Gallery

McGee, Barry
Deitch Projects
Stuart Shave / Modern Ar

McGill, Melissa
CRG Gallery

McGinley, Ryan
Team Gallery

McGinness, Ryan
Deitch Projects

McGrath, Tom
Zach Feuer Gallery

McHargue, Keegan
Hiromi Yoshii
Jack Hanley Gallery
Metro Pictures

McKenna, Stephen
Kerlin Gallery

McKenzie, Lucy
Metro Pictures

McKeown, William
Kerlin Gallery

McLane, Kelly
Angles Gallery
CRG Gallery

McMakin, Roy
Matthew Marks Gallery

McMillian, Rodney
Adamski Gallery for
Contemporary Art

McQueen, Steve
Thomas Dane Gallery

Meadows, Jason
Corvi-Mora
Marc Foxx
Shane Campbell Gallery
Tanya Bonakdar Gallery

Meckseper, Josephine
Arndt & Partner Berlin/Zurich

Media Collective Raqs
Nature Morte

van Meene, Hellen
Marc Foxx

Meese, Jonathan
Galerie Krinzinger
Leo Koenig, Inc.
Stuart Shave/Modern Art

Megerle, Birgit
Daniel Reich Gallery

Mehretu, Julie
The Project
White Cube/Jay Jopling

Meise, Michaela
Greene Naftali
Johann König

Melee, Robert
Andrew Kreps Gallery

Melgaard, Bjarne
Galerie Guido W. Baudach
Galerie Krinzinger
Leo Koenig, Inc.
Sommer Contemporary Art
Stella Lohaus Gallery

Mellor, Dawn
Team Gallery
Victoria Miro Gallery

Mercier, Mathieu
Galerie Chez Valentin

Meromi, Ohad
Harris Lieberman

Merta, Jan
Johnen/Schöttle

Metinides, Enrique
Anton Kern Gallery

Meuser
Meyer Riegger Galerie

Meyerson, Jin
Galerie Emmanuel Perrotin
Zach Feuer Gallery

Mezzaqui, Sabrina
Galleria Continua

Michael, Alan
David Kordansky Gallery
Hotel
Sorcha Dallas
Stuart Shave/Modern Art

Middlebrook, Jason
Sara Meltzer Gallery

Migliora, Marzia
Lia Rumma

Miguel Suro, Luis
Galeria Enrique Guerrero

Mik, Aernout
The Project

Mikhailov, Boris
Galerie Barbara Weiss
Shugoarts

Miklos, Szilard
Plan B

Miko, Dave
Wallspace

Milan, Wardell
Taxter & Spengemann

Milhazes, Beatriz
James Cohan Gallery

Miller, Harland
White Cube/Jay Jopling

Miller, John
Galerie Barbara Weiss
Galerie Praz-Delavallade
Metro Pictures
Meyer Riegger Galerie
Richard Telles Fine Art

Miller, Johnny
Galerie Barbara Thumm

Mineo, Ted
Deitch Projects

Miner, Christopher
Mitchell-Innes & Nash

Minjun, Yue
Arario Gallery

Minter, Marilyn
Andréhn-Schiptjenko
Gavlak

Mir, Aleksandra
Gavlak
greengrassi

Mirra, Helen
Meyer Riegger Galerie

Mischiyev, Igor
GERING & LóPEZ GALLERY

Mishima, Ritsue
Shugoarts

Mitchell, Joan
Cheim & Read
Kukje Gallery

Miyajima, Tatsuo
Lisson Gallery

Miyake, Shintaro
Galerie Krinzinger

Mocafico, Guido
Galerie Kamel Mennour

Mocellin-Nicola Pellegrini, Ottonella
Lia Rumma

Moersch, Stephan
Adamski Gallery for
Contemporary Art

Moretti, Simon
Galerie Chez Valentin

Moffatt, Tracey
Victoria Miro Gallery

Moffett, Donald
Marianne Boesky Gallery

Mohr, Jodie
Black Dragon Society

Moix, Sanit
Paul Kasmin Gallery

Molina, Cortés Domingo
Galerie Gebr. Lehmann

Monahan, Matthew
Anton Kern Gallery
Stuart Shave/Modern Art

Monk, Jonathan
Jack Hanley Gallery
Lisson Gallery
Meyer Riegger Galerie
Yvon Lambert Paris/New York
Casey Kaplan

Monkkonen, Pentti
Black Dragon Society

Monroe, Ian
Haunch of Venison

Monteavaro, Beatriz
Frederic Snitzer Gallery

Montgomery Barron, Jeannette
Magazzino d'Arte Moderna

Moon, Sungsic
Kukje Gallery

Moos, Julie
Fredericks & Freiser

Moppett, Damian
Yvon Lambert Paris/New York

Moran, Katy
Stuart Shave/Modern Art

Moreno, Gean
Frederic Snitzer Gallery

Moretti, Simon
Galerie Chez Valentin

Mori, Chihiro
Kodama

Morimura, Yasumasa
Shugoarts

Moriyama, Daido
Galerie Kamel Mennour
Taka Ishii Gallery

Morlat, Florian
Daniel Hug

Morley, Ivan
Patrick Painter, Inc.

Morris, John
D'Amelio Terras

Morris, Rebecca
Galerie Barbara Weiss
Shane Campbell Gallery

Morris, Sarah
Friedrich Petzel Gallery
Galerie Aurel Scheibler
Galerie Meyer Kainer
White Cube/Jay Jopling

Morrison, Paul
Alison Jacques Gallery
Cheim & Read
Paragon Press

Morton, Victoria
The Modern Institute

Mosbacher, Alois
Galerie Krinzinger

Motti, Gianni
COSMIC Galerie

Moulène, Jean-Luc
Galerie Chantal Crousel
Thomas Dane Gallery

Moulin, Nicolas
Galerie Chez Valentin

Moyer, Carrie
CANADA

Mr.
Galerie Emmanuel Perrotin
Lehmann Maupin

Mthethwa, Zwelethu
Andréhn-Schiptjenko
Jack Shainman Gallery

Mucha, Reinhard
Lia Rumma

Mudzunga, Samson
Michael Stevenson Gallery

Mueck, Ron
James Cohan Gallery

Muehl, Otto
Galerie Krinzinger

Muholi, Zanele
Michael Stevenson Gallery

Mulholland, Craig
Sorcha Dallas

Mull, Carter
Marc Foxx
Rivington Arms

Muller, Dave
Blum & Poe
The Approach

Muller, Matthias
Timothy Taylor Gallery

Müller, Christian-Philipp
Galerie Christian Nagel

Müller, Harald F.
Mai 36 Galerie

Müller, Stefan
Galerie Christian Nagel

Mullican, Matt
Georg Kargl
Mai 36 Galerie

Muñoz, Juan
Galeria Pepe Cobo

Munro, JP
China Art Objects

Muntean/Rosenblum
Arndt & Partner Berlin/Zurich
Galleria Franco Noero
Georg Kargl
Jack Hanley Gallery
Maureen Paley
Team Gallery

Murakami, Takashi
Blum & Poe
Galerie Emmanuel Perrotin
Marianne Boesky Gallery

Murase, Kyoko
Taka Ishii Gallery

Muresan, Ciprian
Plan B

Murphy, John
Lisson Gallery

Murphy, Luke
CANADA

Murray, Elizabeth
PaceWildenstein

Musgrave, David
greengrassi
Marc Foxx

Musil, Barbara
Plan B

Myles, Scott
Jack Hanley Gallery
The Breeder
The Modern Institute

N., Pushpamala
Nature Morte

von Nagel, Augustina
Galeria Pepe Cobo

Naim, Sabah
Lia Rumma

Naito, Rei
D'Amelio Terras

Nakagawa, Torawo
Kodama

Nakahashi, Katsushige
Kodama

Nakao, Hiroko
Victoria Miro Gallery

Nakayama, Daisuke
Kodama

Nakayama, Tracy
Hiromi Yoshii

Nara, Yoshitomo
Blum & Poe
Galerie Meyer Kainer
Johnen/Schöttle
Marianne Boesky Gallery

Nares, James
Paul Kasmin Gallery

Nashashibi, Rosalind
Harris Lieberman

Nashat, Shahryar
Galerie Praz-Delavallade

Nasr, Moataz
Galleria Continua

Nauman, Bruce
Carolina Nitsch

Neel, Alice
Robert Miller Gallery
Victoria Miro Gallery

Nel, Hylton
Michael Stevenson Gallery

Nelson, Mike
Galleria Franco Noero

Neri, Ruby
China Art Objects

Rezac, Richard
Marc Foxx

Rhee, Kibong
Kukje Gallery

Rhoades, Jason
(The Estate of)
Hauser & Wirth Zürich London
David Zwirner

Rhode, Robin
Galerie Kamel Mennour

Riboli, Laura
Wallspace

Richardson, Terry
Galerie Emmanuel Perrotin

Richter, Daniel
David Zwirner

Riddy, John
Frith Street Gallery

Rielly, James
Timothy Taylor Gallery

Rika, Noguchi
D'Amelio Terras

Riley, Bridget
Galerie Aurel Scheibler
PaceWildenstein
Timothy Taylor Gallery

Rischer, Alexander
Adamski Gallery for
Contemporary Art

Rist, Pipilotti
Hauser & Wirth Zürich London

Roach, Damien
Sies + Höke

Robert, Jimmy
Galerie Diana Stigter

Roberts, Julie
Sean Kelly Gallery

Robijns, Gert
Sommer Contemporary Art
Stella Lohaus Gallery

Robleto, Dario
D'Amelio Terras
Galerie Praz-Delavallade

Roccasalva, Pietro
Johnen/Schöttle

Rockburne, Dorothea
Greenberg Van Doren Gallery

Rockenschaub, Gerwald
Galerie Eva Presenhuber
Georg Kargl

Rocklen, Ry
Black Dragon Society

Rockman, Alexis
Leo Koenig, Inc.

Rødland, Torbjørn
Kodama

Rodriguez, Cristina Lei
Galerie Emmanuel Perrotin

Rodriguez, Norberto
Frederic Snitzer Gallery

Roepsorff, Kirstine
Peres Projects

Rogalski, Zbigniew
Galerie Almine Rech

Rogan, Will
Jack Hanley Gallery

Rogers, Brett Cody
David Kordansky Gallery
Galerie Praz-Delavallade
The Approach

Rogers, Les
Leo Koenig, Inc.

Roggan, Ricarda
Galerie EIGEN + ART

Rojas, Clare E.
Deitch Projects
Stuart Shave/Modern Art

Ronay, Matthew
Marc Foxx

Rondinone, Ugo
Galerie Almine Rech
Galerie Eva Presenhuber
Matthew Marks Gallery

Root, Ruth
Andrew Kreps Gallery
Maureen Paley

Rorem, Noah
Shane Campbell Gallery

Rosado, MP & MP
Galeria Pepe Cobo

Rose, Tracey
The Project

Rosefeldt, Julian
Arndt & Partner Berlin/Zurich

Rosen, Kay
Yvon Lambert Paris/New York

Rosenkranz, Pamela
Store

Rosler, Martha
Mitchell-Innes & Nash

Ross, Adam
Angles Gallery

Ross, Alexander
Marianne Boesky
David Nolan Gallery

Rossell, Daniela
Greene Naftali

Rostovsky, Peter
The Project

Roth, Daniel
Hiromi Yoshii
Meyer Riegger Galerie

Roth, Dieter
Carolina Nitsch
Galerie Eva Presenhuber

Rothko, Mark
PaceWildenstein

Rothschild, Eva
303 Gallery
Galerie Eva Presenhuber
galleria francesca kaufmann
Stuart Shave/Modern Art
The Modern Institute

Rough, Gary
Sorcha Dallas

Rousseaud, Bruno
Galerie Almine Rech

Routson, Jon
Team Gallery

Rovner, Michal
PaceWildenstein

Rowe, Heather
D'Amelio Terras

Rozeal Brown, Iona
Sandroni Rey

Rubins, Nancy
Paul Kasmin Gallery

Rubsamen, Glen
Galeria Pepe Cobo
Mai 36 Galerie
Meyer Riegger Galerie

Ruby, Sterling
Foxy Production
Galerie Christian Nagel
Marc Foxx
Metro Pictures

Ruckhäberle, Christoph
Sutton Lane
Zach Feuer Gallery

Rudelius Julika
Galerie Diana Stigter

Ruff, Thomas
David Zwirner
Johnen/Schöttle
Lia Rumma
Mai 36 Galerie

Ruggaber, Karin
greengrassi

Ruilova, Aida
galleria francesca kaufmann
Greenberg Van Doren Gallery
Vilma Gold

Ruscha, Ed
Carolina Nitsch
Patrick Painter, Inc.

Russell, Robert
Anna Helwing Gallery

Rütimann, Christoph
Mai 36 Galerie

Ruyter, Lisa
Arndt & Partner Berlin/Zurich
Galerie Thaddaeus Ropac
Georg Kargl
Team Gallery

Ryan, Anne
greengrassi

Ryman, Robert
PaceWildenstein

Riedel, Michael S.
David Zwirner

Saban, Analia
Galerie Praz-Delavallade

Sachs, Tom
Galerie Thaddaeus Ropac

Saeki, Hiroe
Taka Ishii Gallery

Sæthre, Børre
Galerie Loevenbruck

Sahinler, Murat
Galerist

Sailstorfer, Michael
Jack Hanley Gallery
Johann König

Sala, Anri
Galerie Chantal Crousel
Hauser & Wirth Zürich London
Johnen/Schöttle

Salavon, Jason
Ronald Feldman Fine Arts, Inc.

Salcedo, Doris
White Cube/Jay Jopling

Saldinger, Jeffrey
CRG Gallery

Salisbury, Sam
Alison Jacques Gallery

Salle, David
Galerie Thaddaeus Ropac

Salomone, Yvan
Galerie Praz-Delavallade

Salvino, Andrea
Corvi-Mora

Samaras, Lucas
PaceWildenstein

Sameshima, Dean
Peres Projects
Taka Ishii Gallery

Samson, Justin
John Connelly Presents

Sander, Karin
D'Amelio Terras

Sandison, Charles
Arndt & Partner Berlin/Zurich
Yvon Lambert Paris/New York

Sanditz, Lisa
CRG Gallery

Sanejouand, Jean-Michael
Galerie Chez Valentin

Sanford, Tom
Leo Koenig, Inc.

Saraceno, Tomas
Tanya Bonakdar Gallery

Saret, Alan
James Cohan Gallery

Sarmento, Julião
Galeria Pepe Cobo
Lisson Gallery
Sean Kelly Gallery

Sasnal, Wilhelm
Anton Kern Gallery
Hauser & Wirth Zürich London
Johnen/Schöttle

Sasportas, Yehudit
Galerie EIGEN + ART

Saul, Peter
David Nolan Gallery
Galerie Aurel Scheibler

Saunders, Matt
Galerie Almine Rech
Harris Lieberman

Saunders, Nina
Andréhn-Schiptjenko

Sautour, Stéphane
Galerie Loevenbruck

Saveri, Elizabeth
Shane Campbell Gallery

Saville, Peter
Hotel

Savu, Serban
Plan B

Sawa, Hiraki
James Cohan Gallery

Saylor, Bill
Hiromi Yoshii

Scanlan, Joe
Galerie Chez Valentin

Schachte, Anna
Taxter & Spengemann

Schäfer, Gitte
Galerie Chez Valentin

Scharf, Kenny
Patrick Painter, Inc.
Paul Kasmin Gallery

Schatz, Silke
Meyer Riegger Galerie

Scheibitz, Thomas
Produzentengalerie Hamburg
Tanya Bonakdar Gallery

Scher, David
Leo Koenig, Inc.

Schimert, Katy
David Zwirner

Schindler, Maya
Anna Helwing Gallery

Schink, Claudia
Galerie Aurel Scheibler

Schinwald, Markus
Georg Kargl

Schipper, Jonathan
Pierogi

Schlegel, Eva
Galerie Krinzinger

Schlingensief, Christoph
Hauser & Wirth Zürich London

Schlossberg, Edwin
Ronald Feldman Fine Arts, Inc.

Schmidt, Erik
Galerie Praz-Delavallade

Schmidt, Julia
Casey Kaplan

Schnell, David
Galerie EIGEN + ART
Sandroni Rey

Schnider, Albrecht
Galerie Thomas Schulte

Schnitger, Lara
Anton Kern Gallery
Stuart Shave/Modern Art

Schnyder, Jean-Frédéric
Galerie Eva Presenhuber

Scholl, Dennis
Arndt & Partner Berlin/Zurich

Schomaker, Iris
Galerie Thomas Schulte

Schoorel, Maaike
Galerie Diana Stigter
Marc Foxx
Maureen Paley

Schorr, Collier
303 Gallery
Stuart Shave/Modern Art

Schreuders, Claudette
Jack Shainman Gallery

Schulz, Tilo
Jan Winkelmann/Berlin

Schumann, Christian
Leo Koenig, Inc.
Patrick Painter, Inc.

Schumann, Max
Taxter & Spengemann

Schütte, Thomas
Carolina Nitsch
Frith Street Gallery
Produzentengalerie Hamburg

Schutz, Dana
Zach Feuer Gallery

Schwarzkogler, Rudolf
Galerie Krinzinger

Schwontkowski, Norbert
Kerlin Gallery
Produzentengalerie Hamburg

Scobel, Jenny
Zeno X Gallery

Scognamiglio, Franco
Lia Rumma

Scolnik, Sandra
CRG Gallery

Scully, Sean
Timothy Taylor Gallery

Searle, Berni
Michael Stevenson Gallery

Seawright, Paul
Kerlin Gallery

Séchas, Alain
Galerie Chantal Crousel

Sedira, Zineb
Galerie Kamel Mennour

Segal, Miri
Galerie Kamel Mennour

Sehgal, Tino
Johnen/Schöttle

Selekman, Rachel
Galerie Aurel Scheibler

Selg, Markus
Daniel Hug
Galerie Guido W. Baudach

Seliger, Jonathan
Jack Shainman Gallery

Semans, Macrae
Sandroni Rey
Taxter & Spengemann

Sen, Mithu
Nature Morte

Serebriakova, Maria
Zeno X Gallery

Serrano, Andres
Yvon Lambert Paris/New York

Seward, Lawrence
Andrew Kreps Gallery

Seymen, Erinc
Galerist

Shaobin, Yang
Arario Gallery

Shapero, Mindy
Anna Helwing Gallery
CRG Gallery
The Breeder

Shapiro, Joel
PaceWildenstein

Sharma, Nataraj
Nature Morte

Shaw, Jim
Galerie Praz-Delavallade
Metro Pictures
Patrick Painter, Inc.

Shaw, Raqib
Victoria Miro Gallery

Shawcross, Conrad
Victoria Miro Gallery

Shearer, Steven
Galerie Eva Presenhuber
Galleria Franco Noero
Stuart Shave/Modern Art

Sheldon, Noah
D'Amelio Terras

Shelley, Ward
Pierogi

Sherman, Cindy
Metro Pictures

Shim, Ah-Bin
Kukje Gallery

Shimabuku
Shugoarts

Shipley, Jocelyn
CANADA

Shonibare, Yinka
James Cohan Gallery

Shore, Stephen
303 Gallery
Galerie Kamel Mennour

Shotz, Alyson
Carolina Nitsch

Shows, Leslie
Jack Hanley Gallery

Shrigley, David
Anton Kern Gallery
Yvon Lambert Paris/New York

Shubuck, Simone
Zach Feuer Gallery

Sibony, Gedi
Art : Concept
Johnen/Schöttle

Sidén, Ann-Sofi
Galería Pepe Cobo
Galerie Barbara Thumm

Siekmann, Andreas
Galerie Barbara Weiss

Siena, James
PaceWildenstein

Sierra, Santiago
Lisson Gallery

Sieverding, Katharina
Galerie Thomas Schulte

Signer, Roman
Art : Concept
Galerie Barbara Weiss
Hauser & Wirth Zürich London

Siler, Todd
Ronald Feldman Fine Arts, Inc.

Siltberg, Lars
Milliken

Silva, Cristián
The Project

Silva, Roberta
galleria francesca kaufmann

Simmons, Gary
Metro Pictures

Simmons, Laurie
Carolina Nitsch

Simon Jr., John F.
GERING & LóPEZ GALLERY

Simonson, Susanne
Galleri Magnus Karlsson

Simpson, DJ
Sies + Höke

Simpson, Jane
GERING & LóPEZ GALLERY

Simpson, Lorna
Sean Kelly Gallery

Singh, Dayanita
Frith Street Gallery
Nature Morte

Singh, Diego
Frederic Snitzer Gallery

Skreber, Dirk
Blum & Poe
Friedrich Petzel Gallery

Slaattelid, Mari
Milliken

Slama, Torsten
Hotel

Slimane, Hedi
Galerie Almine Rech

Slominski, Andreas
Metro Pictures
Produzentengalerie Hamburg

Slotawa, Florian
Sies + Höke

Smith, Alexis
Greenberg Van Doren Gallery

Smith, Allison
Bellwether

Smith, Anj
IBID Projects

Smith, Bridget
Frith Street Gallery

Smith, Josh
Hiromi Yoshii

Smith, Kiki
Kukje Gallery
PaceWildenstein
Timothy Taylor Gallery

Smith, Matthew
Store

Smith, Patti
Robert Miller Gallery

Smith, Tony
Hauser & Wirth Zürich London
Matthew Marks Gallery

Smith, Zak
Fredericks & Freiser

Smithson, Robert (The Estate of)
James Cohan Gallery

Snider, Stephanie
Galerie Thomas Schulte

Snow, Dash
Rivington Arms

Snyder, Sean
Galerie Chantal Crousel

Söderberg, Fredrik
Milliken

Solakov, Nedko
Arndt & Partner Berlin/Zurich
Galleria Continua
IBID Projects
Magazzino d'Arte Moderna

Sone, Yutaka
David Zwirner

Sonsini, John
Cheim & Read

Sorensen, Glenn
Annet Gelink Gallery
Corvi-Mora

Sosnowska, Monika
Sommer Contemporary Art
Stella Lohaus Gallery
The Modern Institute

Soulages, Pierre
Robert Miller Gallery

Southwood, Doreen
Michael Stevenson Gallery

Spaans, Dieuwke
Galerie Diana Stigter

Spalletti, Ettore
Galleria Massimo De Carlo

Spangler, Aaron
Zach Feuer Gallery

Spaulings, Reena
Galerie Chantal Crousel
Sutton Lane

Specker, Heidi
Galerie Barbara Thumm

Stadtbäumer, Pia
Sean Kelly Gallery

Stallaerts, Helmut
Johnen/Schöttle

Stark, Frances
CRG Gallery
greengrassi
Marc Foxx

Stark, Linda
Angles Gallery

Starkey, Hannah
Maureen Paley
Tanya Bonakdar Gallery

Starling, Simon
Casey Kaplan
Galleria Franco Noero
The Modern Institute

Stauss, Peter
Galerie Aurel Scheibler

Steckholzer, Martina
Galerie Meyer Kainer

Stehli, Jemima
Lisson Gallery

Steinbach, Haim
Lia Rumma

Steinberg, Saul
PaceWildenstein

Steinbrecher, Erik
Galerie Barbara Weiss

Steinfeld, Daniela
Sara Meltzer Gallery

Steinkamp, Jennifer
Lehmann Maupin

Steir, Pat
Cheim & Read

Stella, Frank
Paul Kasmin Gallery

Stephenson, Clare
Sorcha Dallas

Sternfeld, Joel
Galeria Pepe Cobo

Stevenson, Michael
Vilma Gold

Stewen, Dirk
Tanya Bonakdar Gallery

Stezaker, John
Richard Telles Fine Art
The Approach

Stingel, Rudolf
Galleria Massimo De Carlo
Georg Kargl

Stipl, Richard
Galeria Enrique Guerrero

Stockholder, Jessica
Galerie Thomas Schulte
Mitchell-Innes & Nash

van der Stokker, Lily
galleria francesca kaufmann

Stoltmann, Kirsten
Wallspace

Strachan, Tavares
Pierogi
Ronald Feldman Fine Arts, Inc.

Stratmann, Veit
Galerie Chez Valentin

Strau, Josef
Greene Naftali
Vilma Gold

Strba, Annelies
Frith Street Gallery
Galerie Almine Rech
Galerie EIGEN + ART

Streuli, Beat
Galerie Eva Presenhuber
Galerie Meyer Kainer
Murray Guy

Strid, Anna
Galleri Magnus Karlsson

Strunz, Katja
The Modern Institute

Stumpf, Michael
Sorcha Dallas

Suda, Yoshihiro
D'Amelio Terras

Sugimoto, Hiroshi
Carolina Nitsch
White Cube/Jay Jopling

Sugito, Hiroshi
Arndt & Partner Berlin/Zurich
Marc Foxx

Suh, Do-Ho
Lehmann Maupin

Sullivan, Billy
Galerie Aurel Scheibler
galleria francesca kaufmann

Sullivan, Catherine
Galerie Christian Nagel
Metro Pictures
Richard Telles Fine Art

Sunna, Mari
The Approach

Süßmayr, Florian
Johnen/Schöttle

Suzuki, Tomoaki
Corvi-Mora

Swain, Tony
Herald St
Kerlin Gallery
The Modern Institute

Swallow, Ricky
Stuart Shave/Modern Art

Swansea, Ena
Galerie Crone

Swanson, Marc
Bellwether

Sweeney, Spencer
The Modern Institute

Sweet, Alex
Frederic Snitzer Gallery

Swenson, Erick
James Cohan Gallery

Swoon
Deitch Projects

Szarek, Vincent
Galerie Almine Rech

Sze, Sarah
Marianne Boesky Gallery

Szeemann, Una
Kodama

Tabaimo
James Cohan Gallery

Tait, Neal
Sies + Höke
White Cube/Jay Jopling

Takamine, Tadasu
Kodama

Takano, Aya
Galerie Emmanuel Perrotin

Takemura, Kei
Taka Ishii Gallery

Tallichet, Jude
Sara Meltzer Gallery

Tan, Fiona
Frith Street Gallery

Tanaka, Hidekazu
Kodama

Tàpies, Antoni
PaceWildenstein

Tatah, Djamel
Galerie Kamel Mennour

**Tatham & O'Sullivan,
Joanne & Tom**
The Modern Institute
Sutton Lane

Tauber, Joel
Adamski Gallery for
Contemporary Art

Taylor, Stephanie
Daniel Hug

Taylor-Wood, Sam
White Cube/Jay Jopling

Tayou Pascale, Marthine
Galleria Continua

Tekinoktay, Evren
Galerist
The Approach

Teller, Juergen
Lehmann Maupin

Terada, Mayumi
Robert Miller Gallery

Thater, Diana
David Zwirner
Haunch of Venison
Hauser & Wirth Zürich London

Thauberger, Althea
John Connelly Presents

Thek, Paul
Mai 36

Thiel, Frank
Galerie Krinzinger
Sean Kelly Gallery

Thiel, Stefan
Mai 36 Galerie

Thom, Rob
Black Dragon Society

Thomas, Hank Willis
Jack Shainman Gallery

**Thomkins, André
(The Estate of)**
Hauser & Wirth Zürich London

Thompson, Cheyney
Andrew Kreps Gallery
Sutton Lane

Thomson, Mungo
John Connelly Presents

Thorpe, David
303 Gallery
Maureen Paley
Meyer Riegger Galerie

Thukral & Tagra
Nature Morte

Tichý, Miroslav
David Nolan Gallery

Tillim, Guy
Michael Stevenson Gallery

Tillmans, Wolfgang
Galerie Meyer Kainer
Maureen Paley

Timme, Jan
Galerie Christian Nagel
Marc Foxx

Timoney, Padraig
Andrew Kreps Gallery
The Modern Institute

Tingsgård, Hanna
Milliken

Tiravanija, Rirkrit
Galerie Chantal Crousel

Titchner, Mark
Peres Projects
Vilma Gold

**Tixador & Poincheval,
Laurent & Abraham**
in Situ

Tobias, Gert & Uwe
Team Gallery
The Breeder

Toguo, Barthélémy
Michael Stevenson Gallery

Tokarski, Wawrzyniec
Galerie Jan Wentrup

Tomaselli, Fred
James Cohan Gallery
White Cube/Jay Jopling

Tompkins, Hayley
Andrew Kreps Gallery
Jack Hanley Gallery
The Modern Institute

Tompkins, Sue
The Modern Institute

Torok, Jim
Pierogi

Toroni, Niele
Galerie Barbara Weiss
Yvon Lambert Paris/New York

Toth, Max
Fredericks & Freiser

Trantenroth, Tim
Arndt & Partner Berlin/Zurich

Treleaven, Scott
John Connelly Presents

Tremblay, John
Galerie Almine Rech

Trinkaus, Gabi
Georg Kargl

Trockel, Rosemarie
Galerie Crone
Georg Kargl

Trosch, Thomas
Fredericks & Freiser

Trouvé, Tatiana
Galerie Almine Rech

Trubkovich, Kon
Marianne Boesky Gallery

Tse, Shirley
Murray Guy
Peter Blum Gallery

Tse, Su-Mei
Peter Blum

Tuerlinckx, Joëlle
Sommer Contemporary Art
Stella Lohaus Gallery

Turcot, Susan
Arndt & Partner Berlin/Zurich

Turk, Gavin
Galerie Almine Rech
Galerie Krinzinger
Sean Kelly Gallery
White Cube/Jay Jopling

Turrell, James
Galerie Almine Rech
PaceWildenstein

Tuttle, Richard
Yvon Lambert Paris/New York

Tuttofuoco, Patrick
Bortolami Dayan
Haunch of Venison

Tuymans, Luc
David Zwirner
Zeno X Gallery

Twitchell, Lane
Greenberg Van Doren Gallery

Twombly, Alessandro
Galerie Aurel Scheibler

Tworkov, Jack
Mitchell-Innes & Nash

Tyfus, Dennis
Sommer Contemporary Art
Stella Lohaus Gallery

Tykkä, Salla
Yvon Lambert Paris/New York

Type A
Sara Meltzer Gallery

Tyson, Keith
Haunch of Venison
PaceWildenstein

Tyson, Nicola
Friedrich Petzel Gallery
Marc Foxx

Tzannis, Alexandros
The Breeder

Ufan, Lee
Lisson Gallery

Uklanski, Piotr
Galerie Emmanuel Perrotin
Galleria Massimo De Carlo

Upadhyay, Hema
Nature Morte

Uras, Elif
Galerist
Gavlak

Urdarianu, Veron
Arndt & Partner Berlin/Zurich

Urquhart, Donald
Herald St
Jack Hanley Gallery
Maureen Paley

Uslé, Juan
Cheim & Read
Frith Street Gallery
Galerie Thomas Schulte

Vallance, Jeffrey
Lehmann Maupin

Van Caeckenbergh, Patrick
in Situ
Zeno X Gallery

Van Dongen, Iris
COSMIC Galerie
Galerie Diana Stigter
The Breeder

Vance, Lesley
David Kordansky Gallery

VanDerBeek, Johannes
Zach Feuer Gallery

VanDerBeek, Sara
D'Amelio Terras

Vanga, Gabriela
Plan B

Varejão, Adriana
Lehmann Maupin
Victoria Miro Gallery

Varelas, Jannis
The Breeder

Vasell, Chris
Blum & Poe
Shane Campbell Gallery

Vasquez, Michael
Frederic Snitzer Gallery

Vedovamazzei
Galerie Praz-Delavallade
Magazzino d'Arte Moderna

Vega, Carlos
Jack Shainman Gallery

Veilhan, Xavier
Andréhn-Schiptjenko
Galerie Emmanuel Perrotin
GERING & LóPEZ GALLERY

Venet, Bernar
Robert Miller Gallery

Veoe, Costa
Galleria Franco Noero

Vergara, Angel
Sommer Contemporary Art
Stella Lohaus Gallery

Vergueiro, Nicolau
David Kordansky Gallery

Verhoeven, Helen
Wallspace

Vezzoli, Francesco
Galleria Franco Noero
Yvon Lambert Paris/New York

Villareal, Leo

GERING & LóPEZ GALLERY

Viola, Bill
Haunch of Venison
James Cohan Gallery

Violette, Banks
Maureen Paley
Team Gallery

Visser, Barbara
Annet Gelink Gallery

Vitiello, Stephen
Galerie Almine Rech
The Project

Vitone, Luca
Magazzino d'Arte Moderna

Vlahos, Vangelis
The Breeder

VonMertens, Anna
Jack Hanley Gallery

Vormstein, Gabriel
Casey Kaplan
Meyer Riegger Galerie

Wagner, Philip
Black Dragon Society

Wåhlstrand, Gunnel
Andréhn-Schiptjenko

Walde, Martin
Galerie Krinzinger

Walker, Corban
PaceWildenstein

Walker, Kara
Taka Ishii Gallery

Wall, Jeff
Johnen/Schöttle
White Cube/Jay Jopling

Wallinger, Mark
Galerie Krinzinger

Wang, Suling
Lehmann Maupin
Victoria Miro Gallery

Wapenaar, Dre'
Lia Rumma

Ward, Nari
Deitch Projects

Ware, Chris
Jack Hanley Gallery

Warhol, Andy
Anton Kern Gallery
Galerie Thaddaeus Ropac
Paul Kasmin Gallery
Patrick Painter, Inc.
Ronald Feldman Fine Arts, Inc.

van Warmerdam, Marijke
Galerie Barbara Weiss

Warren, Rebecca
Maureen Paley

Washburn, Phoebe
Zach Feuer Gallery

Wasmuht, Corinne
Meyer Riegger Galerie

Waters, John
Georg Kargl
Marianne Boesky Gallery

Watts, Ouattara
Magazzino d'Arte Moderna

Wearing, Gillian
Maureen Paley

Weatherford, Mary
Shane Campbell Gallery

Webb, Gary
Bortolami Dayan
The Approach

Weber, Klaus
Andrew Kreps Gallery
Herald St

Weber, Marnie
Fredericks & Freiser
Galerie Praz-Delavallade

Weber, Suse
Galerie Gebr. Lehmann

Wedding, Christoph
Galerie Aurel Scheibler

Wei, Li
Patrick Painter, Inc.

Weinberger, Karlheinz
Marc Foxx

Weiner, Lawrence
Lisson Gallery
Mai 36 Galerie
Yvon Lambert Paris/New York

Weir, Mathew
Johnen/Schöttle

Weischer, Matthias
Galerie EIGEN + ART

Weiss, Clemens
Ronald Feldman Fine Arts, Inc.

Weiwei, Ai
Robert Miller Gallery

Welling, James
David Zwirner
Maureen Paley

Wenders, Wim
Haunch of Venison
James Cohan Gallery

Wennerstrand, Per
Galleri Magnus Karlsson

Wentworth, Richard
Lisson Gallery

Wermers, Nicole
Herald St
Produzentengalerie Hamburg
Tanya Bonakdar Gallery

Wesley, Eric
Bortolami Dayan
China Art Objects
Galleria Franco Noero
Meyer Riegger Galerie

Wesley, John
Fredericks & Freiser

Wesselmann, Tom
Robert Miller Gallery

Wesselo, Erik
Annet Gelink Gallery

West, Franz
Galerie Eva Presenhuber
Galerie Meyer Kainer

Westergren, Charlotta
Bellwether

Westphalen, Olav
Milliken

Westwood, Martin
The Approach

Wetzel, Michael
John Connelly Presents

Wexler, Allan
Ronald Feldman Fine Arts, Inc.

Weyer, Anke
CANADA

White, Pae
China Art Objects
galleria francesca kaufmann
greengrassi

White, Tommy
Harris Lieberman

White, Cerasulo John
Sandroni Rey

Whitman, Robert
PaceWildenstein

Whitney, Wallace
CANADA

Wilcox, T.J.
Galerie Meyer Kainer
China Art Objects
Gavlak
Metro Pictures

Wiley, Kehinde
Deitch Projects

Wilhelm, Nay Ernst
Galerie Aurel Scheibler

Wilke, Hannah
Ronald Feldman Fine Arts, Inc.

Wilkes, Cathy
The Modern Institute

Wilkinson, Michael
Daniel Hug
The Modern Institute
Sutton Lane

Willats, Stephen
Galerie Christian Nagel
Victoria Miro Gallery

Willems, Simon
Wallspace

Williams, Bedwyr
Store

Williams, Christopher
David Zwirner
Lia Rumma

Williams, Kelli
Leo Koenig, Inc.

Williams, Sue
David Zwirner
Galerie Eva Presenhuber

Wilson, Amy
Bellwether

Wilson, Fred
PaceWildenstein

Wilson, Ian
Yvon Lambert Paris/New York

Wilson, Jane & Louise
Haunch of Venison
Lisson Gallery
303 Gallery

Winstanley, Paul
Kerlin Gallery
Mitchell-Innes & Nash

Winters, Terry
Matthew Marks Gallery

Wohnseifer, Johannes
Casey Kaplan
Johann König
Yvon Lambert Paris/New York

Wolfson, Jordon
Johann König

Wolgin, Roman
Galerie Diana Stigter
Store

Wong, Yuh-Shioh
Foxy Production

Wood, Jonas
Black Dragon Society

Wood, Tom
The Approach

Woodman, Francesca
Victoria Miro Gallery

Woods, Clare
Stuart Shave/Modern Art

Woods, Richard
COSMIC Galerie

Wool, Chirstopher
Taka Ishii Gallery

Worth, Grant
John Connelly Presents

Wright, Daphne
Frith Street Gallery

Wright, Richard
The Modern Institute

Wu, Peter
Patrick Painter, Inc.

Wulff, Katharina
Greene Naftali

von Wulffen, Amelie
Galerie Crone
Greene Naftali

Wullems, Floor
Annet Gelink

Wurm, Erwin
Galerie Aurel Scheibler
Galerie Krinzinger
Jack Hanley Gallery

Wyn, Evans Cerith
Georg Kargl
White Cube/Jay Jopling

Wyse, Mark
Wallspace

Xhafa, Sislej
Magazzino d'Arte Moderna
Shugoarts
Yvon Lambert Paris/New York

Xiaoyun, Chen
The Project

Xu, Bing
Paul Kasmin Gallery

Yanagi, Miwa
Galerie Almine Rech

Yass, Catherine
Alison Jacques Gallery

Ybarra, Jr. Mario
Anna Helwing Gallery

Yokomizo, Shizuka
The Approach

Yolacan, Pinar
Rivington Arms

Yoneda, Tomoko
Shugoarts

Young, Aaron
Harris Lieberman

Young, Carey
IBID Projects

YP
Kukje Gallery

Yuskavage, Lisa
David Zwirner
greengrassi

Yvoré, Cristof
Zeno X Gallery

Zandvliet, Robert
Peter Blum Gallery

Zaugg, Rémy
Mai 36 Galerie

Zehrer, Joseph
Galerie Christian Nagel

Zeller, Daniel
Pierogi

Zetterquist, Johan
Andréhn-Schiptjenko

Zhao, Gang
Galerie Christian Nagel

Zhen, Chen
Galleria Continua

Zielony, Tobias
Lia Rumma

Zighelboim, Ivette
Marianne Boesky Gallery

Zimmermann, Peter
Galerie Emmanuel Perrotin

Zink Yi, David
Hauser & Wirth Zürich London
Johann König

Zipp, Thomas
Alison Jacques Gallery
Daniel Hug
Galerie Guido W. Baudach
Galerie Krinzinger
Harris Lieberman
Patrick Painter, Inc.
Paragon Press

Zittel, Andrea
Galleria Massimo De Carlo

Ziura, Darius
Magazzino d'Arte Moderna

Zobernig, Heimo
Galerie Christian Nagel
Galerie Meyer Kainer

Zucker, Joe
David Nolan Gallery
Paul Kasmin Gallery
Galerie Aurel Scheibler

Zucker, Kevin
Greenberg Van Doren Gallery

Zybach, Andreas
Johann König

Artist Commission

All stills are from the original video material for *Homo Sapiens Sapiens*, 2005, audio video installation by Pipilotti Rist. The first installation was shown as the Swiss contribution (Bundesamt für Kultur Bern) at the 51st Venice Biennal in the San Stae church in Venice.

Pipilotti Rist commenting on the work: "The figures move in an imaginary paradise beyond thoughts of guilt and seduction. The pictures are from the Garden of Eden before the fall of man (a strange expression in English). I engaged with the meditative rites of the church and the sacred character of Chiesa San Stae. I wanted to show the naked human being* as a philosophical creature by adopting a conception of humanity that is free of original sin in the tradition of representations of paradise. (*In my perception, woman is normal and man is the exception. My naked figures are symbolizing most and first the "human being" and not their gender.)

Different strands of religious fundamentalism all over the world have two things in common: condemnation of the human body and the dogma of a division between body and soul. It is a method for intimidating and controlling people and is invariably coupled with contempt for all things feminine. Double standards, limited education, overpopulation and poverty are the consequences.

I can accept (even if I don't agree) that a group of fundamentalists made a fuss about the installation and made the church close it after 3/4 of the biennale. What really worries me, however, is that these old ideas live on in the heads of most people (even in mine): the naked body is still habitually associated with seduction and guilt. By baring the human body in their works, women artists time and again make explicit the central doctrine of the Church that man – and woman – was created in the image of what they imagine is God. Images are more powerful in their refutation of such ideas than words – I want to capture the strong, self-confident and free human body in its full presence and its vast scope for action. I am looking for heaven on earth, artistically speaking. I want to propose a positive concept that poses an un-dogmatic alternative to hierarchical structures and I want to celebrate liberation in many senses and invent rites."

PIPILOTTI RIST DEEPLY THANKS HER COLLABORATORS:
Performers: Ewelina Guzik, Gry Bay; camera: Pierre Mennel; director assistant: Chris Niemeyer; editing: Davide Legittimo - Videocompany Zofingen; special effects: Edina Gallos-Meyer; green paradies: Bernardo Paz - Caci Centro de Arte Contemporânea Inhotim Brasil, Thiago Gomide; shooting assistance: Mariana Paz, Lucas Sigefredo; sound: Mister Solo Anders Guggisberg - Zentralton Zürich; co-produced by Hauser & Wirth Zürich/London, Cornelia Providoli; line producer: Plan B Film, HC Vogel & Chris Niemeyer.

Thanks for further mental & practical support: Thomas Rhyner, Luhring Augustine NY (Roland, Lawrence & Natalia), Markus Huber Recabarren, Allan Schwartzman, Mauricio Pereira, Jochen Volz, Marc Payot, Ursula Hauser, Iwan & Manuela Wirth, Karinka Seinsoth, Aufdi Aufdermauer & Karin Wegmüller, Käthe Walser, Tamara Rist, Andrea Rist, Rachele Giudici & Balz Roth.

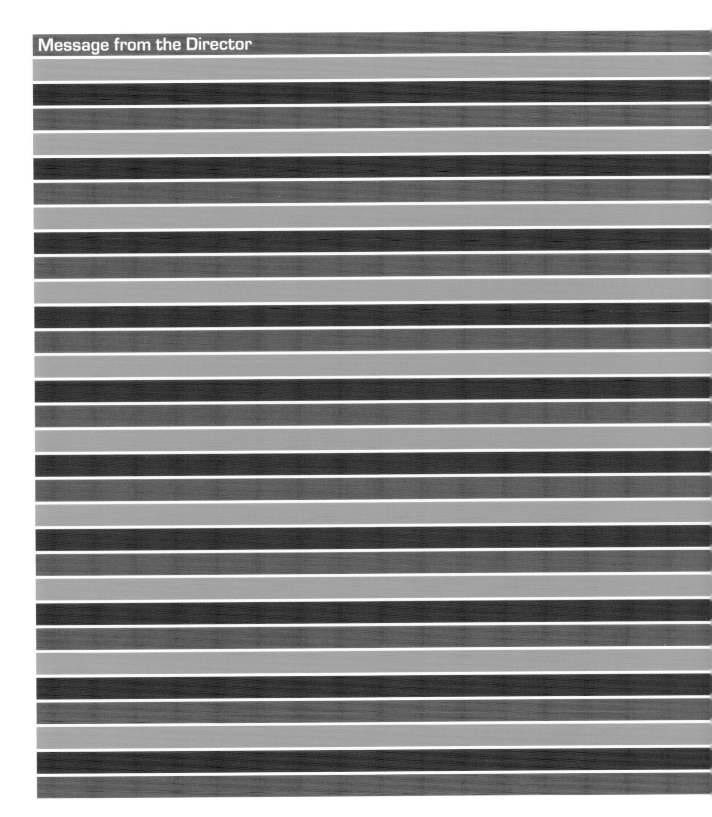

This is my eighth year producing The Armory Show, The International Fair of New Art, and, looking back, I'm amazed by the growing interest in the art world. 8,000 people viewed The Armory Show in 1999 and attendance has risen so dramatically that an artist's work will be seen by 50,000 people during The Armory Show 2007. These viewing numbers were previously only recorded at museums. The Armory Show has effectively become the bridge between the gallery and the mainstream public that artists needed. This is a remarkable achievement and I am honored to have been a part of it. Thank you for joining us.

New York City has come to embrace The Armory Show as a vital community member. The support we receive is a testament to the sophistication and vision of city leaders who understand the power of art to enrich our lives. In particular, I want to thank Mayor Michael R. Bloomberg, City of New York; Speaker Christine C. Quinn, New York City Council; Hon. Daniel L. Doctoroff, Deputy Mayor for Economic Development and Rebuilding; Hon. Kate D. Levin, Commissioner, Department of Cultural Affairs; Kate Ascher, Executive Vice President, New York City Economic Development Corporation; Joan McDonald, Senior Vice President, New York City Economic Development Corporation; and Paul Januszewski, Vice President, New York City Economic Development Corporation.

Pipilotti Rist's singular vision prods us to examine our ideas about our world and ourselves. Her video stills formed a narrative for the fair's visual identity this year and I'm humbled by her generous and kind spirit. The Armory Show has been honored to work with John Wesley (2006), Jockum Nordstrom (2005), Lisa Ruyter (2004), Barnaby Furnas (2003), and Karen Kilimnik (2002). The annual artist commission is an extension of The Armory Show's commitment to new art by living artists.

I learn new things from the gallerists who lend their expertise each year and the 2007 Selection Committee was especially informative. I was impressed by the careful consideration Ciléne Andréhn (Stockholm), Mathias Arndt (Berlin/Zurich), Marc Foxx (Los Angeles), Anton Kern (New York), Emmanuel Perrotin (Paris) and Stuart Shave (London) brought to the process. They are responsible for the outstanding roster of galleries and I applaud their hard work.

The Museum of Modern Art has been an innovative and astute partner, always ready to meet new challenges with us. I especially want to thank Agnes Gund, Jo-Carole Lauder, Glenn Lowry, Michael Margitich, Kim Mitchell and Nicholas Apps. They have been creative in our efforts together and we are proud to have helped them raise millions of dollars to continue their exceptional exhibitions.

This is our third year working with Clifford Chance, our presenting sponsor, and their enthusiasm for and commitment to art sets an example for businesses worldwide. The visionary leadership of Craig Medwick, Americas Regional Partner, and John Carroll has brought contemporary art into the lives of their staff and clients. Amy Goldman, Kendell Kennedy, Cynthia Jacquet, Mary Dinaburg, Susan Reynolds, Jacob Robichaux and Rachel Howe have tirelessly promoted The Armory Show and I want to specially thank them for their support.

Many other sponsors are responsible for The Armory Show 2007 and we could not have produced this edition without them. In particular, Myra Fiori- illy café, Erica Morris- *New York* magazine, Danielle McConnell- *ARTFORUM International*, Jodi Fontana-Vivavi, Jennifer Cibulka and Kristen Ruble- Mandarin Oriental, New York, Jonathan Schwartz- Atelier 4, Lara Shapiro and Kody Gurfein- Quintessentially, Sandy O'Hara- *International Herald Tribune*, Brian Muller- *contemporary* magazine, and Chris Coombes and Chris Jones- artupdate.com.

Roland Augustine, President, and Linda Blumberg, Executive Director, The Art Dealers Association of America, have been inspired partners, wholly dedicated to our collaboration. This is just the beginning. We look forward to expanding our efforts for the benefit of New York, the art world and each of you, our outstanding guests, in the coming years.

The following arts organizations have all generously contributed to our expanding program and we appreciate their support: The Bronx Museum of Arts, The Brooklyn Museum, Asia Society and Museum, Dia:Beacon, El Museo del Barrio, The Solomon R. Guggenheim Museum, International Center of Photography, New Museum of Contemporary Art, MoMA, P.S.1, Noguchi Museum, Queens Museum of Art, Sculpture Center, The Studio Museum in Harlem and the Whitney Museum of American Art.

The Armory Show could not be produced at its current scope and scale without the talent and hard work of a talented group of people who are engaged year round to make it a reality. That group includes Sharon Bar-Lev, Liz Berger, Carol Bouton, Sabrina Buell, Bill Burns, Cristopher Canizares, John D'Amico, Anthony Floreano, William Floyd, G. Bronson Fox, Steven Grasso, Sam Grubman, Elyse Kroll, Gary Lesnevich, Steve Loevsky, Drew McDowall, Mike Morgan, Charles Newman, Stephen Palitz, Mike Perelli, Arianna Petrich, Anna Revchoun, Nicole Tyler Ahlman, Claudia Wagner, and Benjamin Weinman.

Finally, Karen Codd, Pamela Doan, Michael Hall, Manuela Paz and I extend our deepest appreciation to all of our participating galleries. It is their hard work, loyalty and commitment to new art that makes The Armory Show a resounding success.

This and all editions of The Armory Show are dedicated to the loving memory of Pat Hearn and Colin de Land.

—Katelijne De Backer, Director, The Armory Show

The Armory Show 2007—as well as all past and future shows—is dedicated to the loving memory of Pat Hearn and Colin de Land.

Pat Hearn and Colin de Land were leading figures in the contemporary art world for two decades. They were cofounders of both The Gramercy International Art Fair and its successor, The Armory Show, The International Fair of New Art. Tragically, both Pat and Colin died from cancer in their early forties (she in 2000, he in 2003). Two foundations were established to honor their spirit and memory.

The Pat Hearn and Colin de Land Cancer Foundation is a not-for-profit corporation whose mission is to provide assistance for medical expenses to members of the visual arts community suffering from cancer. Financial grants are distributed to cover the costs of medical services, including standard conventional care, unconventional and experimental therapies, palliative care, home care, and hospice care. Further information about the foundation and how to make a contribution is available at www.phcdl.org.

The Pat Hearn and Colin de Land Acquisition Fund at The Museum of Modern Art helps the museum to acquire works in all media by artists who have not received the recognition they deserve. Established in 2000 in Pat Hearn's honor and later renamed in both Pat Hearn and Colin de Land's name, this fund follows the guiding principle that Pat and Colin embraced in their gallery programs, a commitment to new art that lies at the heart of The Armory Show. To learn more about the fund or to make a gift, please contact Emmett S. Watson at The Museum of Modern Art by phone, 212.708.9404, or email emmett_watson@moma.org.

ARTISTS AND POETS ARE THE
RAW NERVE ENDS OF HUMANITY
BY THEMSELVES THEY CAN DO LITTLE
TO SAVE HUMANITY
WITHOUT THEM THERE WOULD BE
LITTLE WORTH SAVING

JIMMY ERNST

In 2006 The Armory Show began publishing an annual series of editions to benefit the two foundations as an extension of The Armory Show's distinguished annual artist commission. John Wesley was the first artist to support the funds. Last year, Wesley donated two silkscreen prints to this project; this year, Pipilotti Rist, who accepted The Armory Show 2007 commission, has generously donated two photographic editions.

To purchase these works please contact The Armory Show office at info@thearmoryshow.com.

Pipilotti Rist
Small Homo Plants Herself, Kleiner Mensch planzt sich hin
2006
Video still, ink print on rag paper
Image: 17 x 13 ¾ inches; 43 x 35 cm
sheet: 23 ¼ x 16 ½ inches; 59 x 42 cm
Edition of 30 + 10 AP
Courtesy the artist, Hauser & Wirth Zurich London
and Luhring Augustine Gallery, New York.

Pipilotti Rist
Small Homo Toes The Line, Kleiner Mensch ist zu einem Vorhaben bereit
2006
Video still, ink print on rag paper
Image: 17 x 13 ¾ inches; 43 x 35 cm
sheet: 23 ¼ x 16 ½ inches; 59 x 42 cm
Edition of 30 + 10 AP
Courtesy the artist and Hauser & Wirth Zurich London
and Luhring Augustine Gallery, New York.